ANGRY CLASSROOMS

VACANT MINDS

What's Happened to Our High Schools?

ANGRY CLASSROOMS

VACANT MINDS

*What's Happened to
Our High Schools?*

Martin Morse Wooster

PACIFIC RESEARCH INSTITUTE FOR PUBLIC POLICY
San Francisco, California

ISBN 0-936488-74-3

Printed in the United States of America
10   9   8   7   6   5   4   3   2   1

PACIFIC RESEARCH INSTITUTE FOR PUBLIC POLICY
755 Sansome Street, Suite 450
San Francisco, CA 94111
(415) 989-0833

Library of Congress Cataloging-in-Publication Data
Wooster, Martin Morse, [date]
    Angry classrooms, vacant minds: what's happened to our high schools? / Martin Morse Wooster
        p.   cm.
    Includes bibliographical references (p.) and index.
    ISBN 0-036488-74-3
    1. Education, Secondary—United States—History. 2. School management and organization—United States—History.
3. Educational change—United States—History. I. Title.
LA222.W66   1994   93-34168
373.73—dc20   CIP

Director of Publications: *Kay Mikel*
Cover Design: *Arrowgraphics*
Index: *Shirley Kessel, Primary Sources Research*
Printing and Binding: *Edwards Brothers Inc.*

CONTENTS

Preface / *ix*

PREFACE

This book describes American public high schools in two ways—as a social history and as a synthesis of hundreds of books, articles, and monographs about American education. It is not meant to advance an agenda or to end arguments.

I certainly have opinions about the schools, but I have tried to keep them out of this book as much as possible and have strived to be accurate in describing views with which I disagree. It is my hope that this book will be useful to parents, teachers, and concerned citizens who want to learn about the problems of American education but do not have the time or the patience to read all the books about the schools that I have read.

Most books about American secondary education begin by telling the readers about how terrible the schools are and then offer a short list of reforms. But whether written by liberals or conservatives, these books don't tell you *why* American high schools are the way they are. That's because most writers on education have little sense of the past. An average education book may give its readers a few paragraphs about the nineteenth century and a glancing reference to the idea that someone, some time ago, thought that a school should be like a factory. But nearly all education writers assume that the history of America's schools is not very interesting; these writers rarely describe events in American education prior to 1965.

I begin with a different premise. If you understand the history of American education, you'll know more about the problems teachers, principals, and parents face than do nearly all the pundits. The reason the United States, unlike most other democracies, has a national system of privately funded parochial schools is the result of a riot that took place in Philadelphia more than 150 years ago. A doctoral dissertation published seventy-five years ago resulted in creation of central offices that micromanage the schools to this day. And the current debate on whether students preparing for blue-collar careers should train in schools or in businesses duplicates arguments made eighty years ago—arguments that resulted in creation of the vocational education system that the Clinton administration wishes to transform.

My book begins by exploring the debates in America over whether or not secondary education should be private or public. I begin with the Philadelphia Bible Riots of 1842, which ensured that Catholic schools would be private and separate from Protestant-dominated public schools. Then I trace the debate over whether or not private schools would continue to exist, a debate concluded by the Supreme Court in the *Pierce* decision of 1925, which ensured that private parochial schools were constitutional, provided they were subject to government regulation. Next, I look at how public schools began to change in the 1920s as a result of the progressive education movement, which made schools more centralized and more prone to teach courses that were less academic than in previous generations. The progressive educationists were succeeded in the 1950s by the more conservative "basic education" movement, which then was superseded in the 1960s by a new generation of progressives. I conclude by looking at the growth of federal aid in education, beginning with the failure of Harry S Truman to establish a federal Department of Education in the 1940s, continuing with the growth in federal aid as a result of the Great Society program of the 1960s, and ending with creation of the Department of Education in 1978. But the inertia of the 1980s and 1990s, when Democrats in Congress had enough power to preserve programs but not enough clout to add to them, ensured that the Department of Education would stagnate in the 1970s and 1980s. Very little changed in the Department of Education between the time Jimmy Carter left the presidency in 1981 and Bill Clinton became president in 1993; this stagnation ensured that educational change would be the result of state and local action, not a result of any federal effort.

Chapter 2 explores the problem of what sort of moral principles, if any, should be taught in the classroom. In 1900 most public schools taught a Bible-based morality that was superseded by the rise of social science in the first quarter of the twentieth century, which resulted in a national movement of "character education." Character education was discredited as a result of a study conducted by Columbia University in the late 1920s that showed that most character education classes not only did not teach students right from wrong but may have made students more immoral by cheating on good conduct records.

The debate over moral education subsided until the 1960s, when two schools of thought emerged about the best way to teach children right and wrong. The "values clarification" movement, strongly influenced by the ideas of psychologist Carl Rogers, held that morality could not be taught but that teachers could guide students to discover moral beliefs. The "just community" movement, led by Harvard psychologist Lawrence Kohlberg, held that everyone passes through six stages of moral development and that the teacher's role was to lead students to the highest stage, where they would use such abstract principles as the Golden Rule and the categorical imperative. But by the 1970s, both movements had died out; scholars showed that the values clarification movement had little effect on students' thinking. After a failed attempt to create a just community, Lawrence Kohlberg largely repudiated his views on moral development.

Today, many teachers are using character education models very much like those used in the 1920s. But the revived character education movement is probably less able to help children than in the past, because of the diminished authority most adults have in the lives of high school students. In my opinion, the best way teachers can help students become decent and just is if teachers become good examples to their students and if students study great works of literature instead of bland "basal readers."

In chapter 3 I look at the principal's changing role. Most education reformers argue that schools will not improve until principals become leaders instead of middle managers taking orders from the central office and passing reports up the organizational chain. Both James S. Coleman and Thomas Hoffer's *Public and Private High Schools* (1987) and John Chubb and Terry Moe's *Politics, Markets, and American Schools* (1990) show that public high schools where principals have a relatively free hand in shaping a school's corporate culture have students who achieve more than schools where principals are largely bound by orders from above.

But principals were never wholly independent actors, and complaints that the principal's authority was being restricted are quite old. As early as 1913 Stanford education professor Ellwood P. Cubberley studied the Portland, Oregon, schools and found that principals were required to follow eight pages of rules, including the requirement that they be at their schools one hour early in case of cold weather.

Until the 1960s, principals had a great deal of freedom in shaping their schools. But the rise of the two national teachers' unions ensured that many questions in schools would be made by the union contract, not the principal. (The ultimate result of teachers' union power was to make schools more rigid and inflexible than they were before unions gained the clout they have today.) The rise of support staff—pregnancy-prevention counselors, drug treatment staffers, special education instructors—whose salaries were paid by state or federal government grants, further reduced the principal's power. Supreme Court decisions designed to enhance students' rights, such as *Tinker v. Des Moines* (1969) and *Goss v. Lopez* (1975) ensured that courts and judges would make decisions that principals once made. And the reforms instituted in the wake of the publication of *A Nation at Risk* in 1983—tougher graduation requirements, longer school days, more homework, stricter teacher certification—did little to help principals who were given no say in how these reforms were to be carried out. Without some devolution of power, either via school-based management, charter schools, or school choice, principals are not likely to regain the power they have steadily lost.

Chapter 4 looks at the problems teachers face. Over the past half-century, the authority of the American high school teacher has steadily waned: students have become bored, impudent, and less willing to learn; administrators smother teachers in red tape and fail to assist them in discipline matters; and regulations created by distant, autocratic state and local school boards make teachers' jobs steadily more demanding, more frustrating, and less interesting.

But this decline in authority is not new. Far too many students were as uninterested in learning in the 1920s as in the 1990s. In 1924, for example, when Robert S. Lynd and Helen Staughton Lynd studied the high school in the city they called Middletown, they found that academic classes were being replaced by "practical" ones and that teachers were not the "wise, skilled, revered elders" they once were.

But it wasn't until the 1960s that teaching began to be transformed, as thousands of nontraditional teachers flooded the schools. Many of these teachers, having read John Holt and Jonathan Kozol, listened to Jefferson Airplane or Bob Dylan, or watched *To Sir, With Love,* attempted to radically transform the schools. The result was to destroy the informal moral consensus that had governed public schools and replace it with what sociologist Gerald Grant calls "a more impersonal legal-bureaucratic order." The decisions teachers made were no longer based primarily on whether a student's action was right or wrong but on whether a student act violated federal statutes and district regulations.

Faced with schools that were more bureaucratic and less pleasant than in the past, many teachers fled the classroom. The term *burnout* was not in use in 1960 (it appears to have been coined by Graham Greene in his 1961 novel *A Burnt-Out Case*), but by 1975 teacher burnout was commonplace. The teachers who survived were increasingly frustrated, and many were less willing to inspire students to work hard. By the 1980s, "the shopping mall high school" was commonplace. Schools, like malls, had become places to sample products at the students' leisure, where a good education was still possible but where few adults were eager (or even interested) in having students strive toward excellence. And central offices were places where regulations were created on the premise that teachers were incompetent and needed to be governed, restricted, and ruled. The result was a self-fulfilling prophecy: Teachers, hampered by red tape and burdened by endless rules, have been far less effective than they would have been if left to their own devices.

Chapter 5 shows how schools become centralized. Until 1900, America's schools were relatively decentralized; in 1890, for example, the average state department of education had two employees; nearly 500,000 local school boards hired and fired employees and largely controlled American secondary education. But these "ward boards" were systematically destroyed as a consequence of the Progressive movement. The Progressives believed that government organizations should be governed by nonpartisan executives committed to the public interest as opposed to partisan politicians committed to advancing the viewpoint of a particular party or faction. The Progressives believed that a small school board and a strong superintendent would do more to improve schools than decentralized ward boards.

By 1915, the Progressives completed their program of school centralization. In city after city, the school board shrank and the superintendent gained more power. But it took a graduate student at Columbia University's Teachers College to come up with the other permanent feature of school centralization—the central office.

For his dissertation, J. Howard Hutchinson visited various school systems and found that few of them could describe how they ordered supplies or how many goods they had in stock. He recommended that school districts adopt twenty-two forms, including purchase orders, time sheets, and expense ledgers. School superintendents seized on this idea, as it was a relatively low-cost way to show citizens how their tax dollars were being spent.

So by 1920 the structure and organization of American schools were set in ways that continue today. The superintendent, seeing himself as powerful as the chief executive of a large corporation, usually insisted on a hierarchical school system using managerial techniques (such as command-and-control or line-and-staff management) thought innovative at the time. School districts were to have large central offices that restricted the autonomy of schools by restricting supplies and by minutely regulating conduct and school governance. Had these superintendents chosen alternative models of organization (such as those used in hospitals or churches), schools might have stayed decentralized and superintendents might have thought of themselves as scholars rather than accountants. But that was not to happen.

But the superintendent's power was to steadily weaken over time. The changes in schools that resulted from the *Brown* decisions of 1954 and 1955 ensured that courts would, in many cities, take away the superintendent's power. The rise of the teachers' unions in the 1960s weakened superintendents in much the same way that it weakened principals. Federal mandates resulting from the large increase in education funding during the Johnson and Nixon administrations further restricted the superintendent. The revisions in schools resulting from the reforms of 1983 to 1986 took still more power away from superintendents and placed it in the hands of state or federal bureaucrats further removed from the schools. Today a superintendent is the civil service equivalent of a baseball manager—praised when things go well, swiftly fired when problems erupt. As a result, there are many vacancies for superintendents and few applicants. At one point in early 1993, the nation's three largest school systems— Los Angeles, New York, and Chicago—were all looking for superintendents.

Chapter 6 continues the story by looking at ways that schools can be decentralized. Experiments at school decentralization are nearly as old as those of school centralization; they begin with superintendent Ella Flagg Young's attempts in Chicago in the 1890s to create teacher councils that routinely gave advice to higher levels of the school bureaucracy. These efforts were crushed and forgotten, but a similar notion was attempted in the 1970s with the creation of programs of "school-based management." It is not certain that school-based management actually devolves power; evidence from several cities (particularly Salt Lake City) shows that this reform is not only hard to define but may well result in more, not less, bureaucracy and far too often excludes parents from any positions of importance. The reforms in Chicago's schools that give councils of parents, teachers, and concerned citizens some power to control budgets and hire and fire principals may prove more beneficial, but evidence of their effectiveness is weak and inconclusive.

Two other school decentralization proposals appear more

promising. As a result of the Education Reform Act of 1988, British schools were given the option of either controlling 85 percent of their budgets or "opting out" and controlling 100 percent of their budgets. This appears to have given a great deal of autonomy to schools. (School autonomy, however, was reduced by another provision of the act that implemented a national curriculum.) The charter schools being created in Minnesota, California, and other states may also provide a way for schools to gain more freedom from arbitrary restrictions and red tape.

Chapter 7 looks at education's most controversial reform, school choice. Choice is also an old reform. Adam Smith, John Stuart Mill, and Thomas Paine all favored school choice; Paine even encouraged a reform that was very much like a school voucher. The opposition to school choice is also quite old. Puerto Rico and thirty-seven states ban public funds being used for private schools because of an effort begun by Speaker of the House James G. Blaine in 1874.

The school choice story begins in the 1950s, as eight southern states attempted to defy the Supreme Court's *Brown* decisions by creating segregationist "schools of choice" or "free choice" plans. These plans were eliminated by the Supreme Court in *Green v. New Kent County* (1968), which ruled free choice plans unconstitutional. So a school choice plan, if it was to take place, would have to meet federal integration guidelines.

One promising idea was the school voucher, invented by Milton Friedman in a 1955 paper. In the late 1960s, Harvard sociologist Christopher Jencks and his associates adopted the school voucher in a proposal quite similar to that proposed by John Chubb and Terry Moe nearly twenty years later. Jencks's proposal, which would have given more money to low-income parents than the better off, was barely put to the test; after many large cities and states refused to allow a voucher experiment, only the small town of Alum Rock, California, attempted to use vouchers. The results of the Alum Rock experiment were inconclusive and are still debated nearly twenty years after the voucher test was tried.

Except for Alum Rock and the programs in Milwaukee (only available to 1 percent of that city's children), we have no

U.S. data about whether or not vouchers will transform schools, but some evidence is available from programs in Canada and England. Studies conducted by Donald Erickson of the University of California (Los Angeles) of Canadian government aid to parochial schools shows that these schools became less independent and more like public schools as government subsidies increased. The English "assisted-places" scheme, which provides subsidies for working class parents to enable their children to attend private schools, has helped English children somewhat. But Tony Edwards and his associates at the University of London, in an exhaustive analysis of the assisted-places program, concluded that the plan did little to help the children of poor parents climb the social ladder; most of the parents who participated in the plan were from relatively well-educated households where incomes were depressed because of disability, unemployment, or divorce. (Forty percent of the assisted-place scheme families were single-parent households.) This evidence suggests that the effect of vouchers on schools will be more gradual and less dramatic than either friends or foes of the reform suppose.

We also know that the Supreme Court will rule in any voucher plan that includes parochial schools. To understand how the Supreme Court might rule on vouchers, we need to examine the Court's past rulings on parochial schools, rulings so convoluted that, at one point in the mid-1970s, the court ruled that it was constitutional for the government to loan textbooks to parochial schools (*Board of Education v. Allen*, 1968) but unconstitutional for the government to loan the same schools maps, nonreligious periodicals, and laboratory equipment (*Meek v. Pittenger*, 1975). Given that most Supreme Court decisions about aid to parochial schools have been narrow decisions that have not split along standard liberal–conservative lines, it could well be that the Court will declare vouchers constitutional—or constitutional only in states where parochial schools are a minority of all private schools.

I also include a discussion of public school choice: its invention by Mario Fantini in the early 1970s, its implementation as "controlled choice programs" in some cities (particularly, Cambridge, Massachusetts) seeking alternatives to school busing, and its revival in Minnesota and other states seeking choice without vouchers. While I believe that public school choice may help schools, it is very much like school-based management—it can be reversed at any time for any reason. Without assurances that public school choice will be permanent and lasting, the reform could either fail or be watered down in such a way that it will produce no beneficial effects.

The book ends with an extensive bibliography of books and articles on education—histories, research reports, and the occasional manifesto. I believe these are the most innovative, interesting, and provocative studies on education that have been written in the past twenty-five years.

Acknowledgments

The book was funded via a grant from The Educational Reviewer, Inc., via *National Review*. My supervisor for this project, Patricia Bozell, also edited the book. Trish Bozell is a judicious supervisor and a superb editor; it was a pleasure to work with her. At the Pacific Research Institute for Public Policy, Kay Mikel did a fine job copy editing and producing this book.

Portions of the book have been published elsewhere. Chapter 2 first appeared in *The American Enterprise*. Chapter 3 was first published in *Policy Review*. Part of chapter 6 was published in *Reason*. Thanks to Adam Meyerson, Karlyn Bowman, and Virginia Postrel both for publishing me and for their editorial advice.

Most of this book was researched at the Library of Congress and at the U.S. Department of Education Library. Several staff members of the U.S. Department of Education provided valuable suggestions. Nelson Smith helped with the research for the chapter on principals. Jack Klenk and his colleagues at the Center for Choice in Education provided many documents and studies about school choice. Stephen Sniegoski of the Department of Education Library and I had many discussions about the history of education. William Hussar of the National Center for Education Statistics helped me interpret and analyze education statistics.

Many people across the nation also helped me in the project. Patrick Keleher of TEACH America patiently assisted me in understanding Chicago's educational problems. John McClaughry provided assistance in discussing the history of school choice in Vermont. James Bowman taught me a good deal about British schools. In the book's last stages, Colin Walters of the *Washington Times* suggested that I write a column reviewing education books; several of the books sent for review are cited in these pages. Other documents, suggestions, or encouragement were provided by Sir Rhodes Boyson, Richard Burr, Bruce Cooper, Bruce Duffy, Rodger Morrow, and Lawrence Uzzell.

Martin Morse Wooster
Silver Spring, Maryland
October 1993

"There is, I am confident, much more autocracy on the part of superintendents and principals in public schools than by presidents and deans in colleges. Our lower schools are ridden by 'administrators'; they are administration-mad. An arm's length efficiency, conducted by typewriters from central offices, reaches into the classrooms where all the educational work is done and produces there the inefficiency of irresponsibility and routine. Yet these things mostly go without comment."
John Dewey, *School and Society*, January 7, 1928.

"The danger of Federal assistance to public schools is not the source of the money but the predictable incorporation of such assistance in both established and emerging bureaucracies, which, like most bureaucracies, especially at the lowest levels, will make fidelity to the letter of the law a transcending objective, making it even more difficult to keep alive the spirit within which good teaching alone can thrive."
Robert Nisbet, *The Quest for Community: A Study in the Ethics of Order and Freedom* (San Francisco, CA: Institute for Contemporary Studies, 1990), p. xxviii-xxix.

ANGRY CLASSROOMS

VACANT MINDS

1

A SHORT HISTORY OF AMERICAN EDUCATION

To understand the nature of the problems currently confronting high schools, we first need to show how these problems came to be. To do this, a short historical survey of American high schools is in order.

Until about 1850, the line of demarcation between "private" and "public" high schools was not clear. In New York City, for example, the public schools were controlled until 1853 by a private organization, the Free School Society of New York. Although the Free School Society was subsidized largely through taxes (mainly liquor and real estate fees), it distributed its budget to Protestant, Catholic, and secular schools without preference. Few Americans believed in spending much government money on education; even Thomas Jefferson, whose faith in education was unmatched by any of the other Founders, only believed in state-supported primary schools. (Jefferson thought that secondary schools should, like New York City's schools, be privately managed and receive limited public funds.)

The birth of the "common-school movement" ended the compromise between public and private schools. As historian

Lloyd Jorgenson notes, common-school advocates tended to be Whigs who generally favored the growth of centralized government and thus supported "internal improvements" to America's roads, protectionism, a national bank, and increased government spending on education.[1]

Common-school advocates, according to historian Lawrence Cremin, "shared a common belief in a millennial Christian republican economy in which education would play a central role."[2] They tended to be liberal Protestant ministers who proselytized the faith of mass education with messianic fervor. Horace Mann, for example, noted in the 1848 annual report of the Massachusetts Board of Education that "the common school is the greatest discovery ever made by man. . . . Let the common school be expanded to its capabilities, let it be worked with the efficiency of which it is susceptible, and nine tenths of the crimes in the penal code would become obsolete."[3]

Other common-school advocates had darker motives for supporting public education—attacking Catholics. One W. W. Turner, for example, told the Connecticut branch of the American Education Society in 1835 that common schools were necessary because "multitudes of foreign papists are every year pouring in upon our shores, bringing with them all the passions and prejudices of a foreign education."[4]

A number of American ministers visited Catholic schools in Europe, but they used their visits simply to reconfirm their prejudices. "Frivolity, sensuality, and the Catholic religion," observed Horace Mann after a tour of German parochial schools in 1843, "What will they do for the debasement of mankind?"[5]

Thus the ministers who became state or city superintendents of schools in America between 1835 and 1855 tended to be Protestant centralists devoted to expanding education. Rev. Birdsley Grant Northrup, a Methodist who became Connecticut's superintendent of schools in the 1850s, invented the property tax as a method of paying for schools. (Before this time, public school taxes usually consisted of a "rate bill," in which parents were charged a fee based on the number of children they had in school at any given time.)

In an anti-Catholic effort in Philadelphia, Protestants in

2

charge of the school curriculum convinced their legislatures to pass laws mandating daily Bible reading from a King James Bible. But Catholic priests insisted that students from their congregations be allowed to read from the Douay Bible; when school boards refused, Catholic parents began to withdraw their students from the public schools and place them in newly formed Catholic schools.

Philadelphia school board members faced a problem. How could they enforce mandatory attendance in public schools *and* King James Bible reading? At first, the school board declared that any student who objected to the King James Bible would be given a Bible of their choice, but without "notes or comment." But Catholics found this decision objectionable, since the footnotes to the Douay Bible contained valuable Catholic teaching, and a Bible without commentary was not a Catholic one. So the Catholics began to withdraw their children from Bible classes; the Philadelphia schools thus offered two types of education—a Protestant education, and a secular one for Catholics.

At the same time, anti-immigrant forces in Philadelphia saw the Bible controversy as a plot by foreigners to destroy America. The American Republican Association, for example, was founded in 1843 with a three-point platform: 21-year residency requirements for citizenship, a ban on any naturalized citizen holding public office, and daily readings in the schools from the King James Bible.

Throughout 1843 and 1844, these American nativists (who called themselves "native Americans") continued to agitate against Catholics. On May 6, 1844, the nativists—3000 strong— held a rally to "save the Bible" in Kensington, then (as now) a white working-class section of Philadelphia. In the middle of the rally, Catholics stormed the stage with wheelbarrows and dumped mud on the platform. This led to a fight in which two Protestant children died, an event that began the "Philadelphia Bible Riots."

The next day, Protestant boys marched through Kensington's streets with a tattered flag and a banner reading "this is the flag that was trampled under foot by Irish papists." Outraged nativists retaliated by burning more than 30 Catholic homes. The following day the Philadelphia *Daily Sun*, a leading nativist organ, published an editorial that offered its commentary on the conflicts between Protestants and Catholics. "We write at this moment," said the *Daily Sun* editorialist, "with our garments stained and sprinkled with the blood of victims—the rights of conscience—the rights of persons—the holy safeguards and privileges of freedom. Yes, we write with our garments sprinkled with the precious life drops of martyrs to freedom."

This editorial ensured that the Bible riot would spread beyond Kensington as dozens of churches and homes were put to the torch. Protestants found that the only way their homes could be saved was by placing large signs in their lawns that read "NATIVE AMERICAN."

The Philadelphia Bible Riots finally ended with the intervention of the state militia and at least one U.S. warship. The riots not only caused 14 deaths and a massive amount of property damage but also ensured that the common school would not be something every American would experience.[6]

By the end of the 1840s, Protestants controlled most state public school systems. But by their prejudice against Catholics and their desire for universal school attendance, these Protestants also ensured that any alternatives to the public school system would be private, not public. During this same period, several European nations, on the other hand, were implementing systems of public education that allowed choice within public schools.

In the Netherlands, as an example, public schools were first established in the early nineteenth century by Protestants who, like their counterparts in America, wanted to teach nondenominational Protestantism to all students. (Historian Charles Glenn notes that Horace Mann described the "inoffensive religious teaching" favored by the Dutch of the time as an example he wished Americans could follow.[7]) After the revolution of 1848, which caused radical forces to advance in the Netherlands in much the same way they advanced in Germany, Austria, and France, the anti-clerical Liberal Party dominated Dutch politics and tried various strategies to check the growth of Roman Catholic and Calvinist private schools, culminating in an 1878 law that

4

banned all public subsidies to private schools. But the Dutch Roman Catholic and Calvinist political parties fought back, gaining a majority in the 1888 elections. In 1889 the Dutch Parliament passed a law that declared that all schools, both public and parochial, receive 30 percent of their budgets from the national government. Article 23 of the Netherlands' constitution guarantees that any school created by parents will be funded by the state as long as the government certifies the quality of the school and approves the moral character of the teachers. Thus all schools in the Netherlands are state funded but most are run either by foundations or church-related organizations. In 1980, for example, 20.7 percent of all Dutch students were in state-run secondary schools, but the remaining 79.3 percent were in privately run, state-subsidized schools—24.8 percent in Protestant schools, 36.8 percent in Catholic schools, and the remaining 17.7 percent in nondenominational private schools.

A roughly similar process occurred in Canada, where Methodist minister Egerton Ryerson (the Canadian counterpart to Horace Mann) encouraged the growth of public schools in Canada from the 1850s onward. But unlike America, these schools from their origins were declared by the state to be either Protestant or Catholic; for over a century, most Canadian Catholic schools have been state-funded with parents free to choose the school of their choice. Only in January 1990 did the Supreme Court of Canada declare the nation's Protestant schools to be "secular;" parents are currently lobbying to allow Christian, non-Catholic schools to receive public funds.[8]

Back in America, the relative political weakness of Catholics ensured that they would have to create their own schools, and that these schools would not be state funded. Thus the question of choice in American education became one of choosing either public or private education, not of choosing alternatives within public education.

But although the number of private schools were small, many public school educators still saw them as formidable competitors whose activities should be restricted as much as possible. In the 1860s and 1870s, some cities attempted to take over private schools by coercion or subsidies. During this period, some states

5

and cities attempted to merge parochial and public school systems. In Poughkeepsie, New York, Catholic schools were actually operated by the public schools between 1873 and 1898, a merger that only ended when the New York state school superintendent ruled that nuns and priests could not wear clothing signifying their faith in the classroom. A similar merger was implemented in Fairbault and Stillwater, Minnesota, between 1891 and 1893; it was ended by Catholics who feared that religious teachings would erode in state-run Catholic schools. In New York City, Boss Tweed tried, but failed, to implement parochial school subsidies as a vote-getting measure. But these threats were overturned, and Catholic schools in the few cities where mergers occurred reverted to their separate status.

In the 1870s, opponents of Catholic schools, in another attempt to ensure the dominance of public schools, tried to create a national department of education. In 1871, Sen. Henry Wilson (R-Pennsylvania), in an influential article in *The Atlantic Monthly*, said that a national department of education was needed to ensure that U.S. schools avoid the fate of "ignorant, priest-ridden, and emasculated France."[9] And in 1882, Sen. Henry Blair (R-New Hampshire) introduced a bill creating a U.S. Department of Education, which passed the Senate three times between 1882 and 1886. But Blair's bill was never considered by the House of Representatives, and Senator Blair became increasingly deranged, publicly accusing newspapers of being part of a "Jesuit conspiracy" against him and threatening to ban all reporters from the Senate unless he were given better coverage. The proposed "department of education" became as discredited as its sponsor.

In 1922, foes of parochial schools made one last effort to deny choice in education. In the state of Oregon, voters approved, by a narrow margin, a referendum backed by the Ku Klux Klan in alliance with some Masonic lodges that required students to attend public schools unless a school superintendent allowed them to attend a private school. Defending the common school, said the King Kleagle (Pacific Domain) of the Knights of the Ku Klux Klan, "is the settled policy of the Ku Klux Klan and with its white-robed sentinels keeping eternal watch it shall for all time... cry out the warning when danger appears and take its place in the front rank of defenders of public schools."[10]

Prominent Catholics across America denounced the referendum; Archbishop Austin Dowling of St. Paul, Minnesota, said that the Oregon referendum was equivalent to "the Soviet claim to invade the home and substitute communal for parental care."[11] "The whole trend of such legislation is state socialism," added Archbishop Michael Curley of Baltimore.[12]

Non-Catholics (particularly Baptists) also denounced the decision; they were joined by such prominent Americans as the presidents of Yale, Columbia University, and the University of Texas, the American Civil Liberties Union, the National Education Association, and at least one former U.S. Commissioner of Education. Even John Dewey attacked the Oregon decision.

In Oregon, an order of nuns began an effort to overturn the decision, which reached the Supreme Court in 1925. In *Pierce v. the Society of Sisters*, the Court declared private schools constitutional and overturned the Oregon ban. The Court's decision was eloquent:

> *The fundamental theory of liberty upon which all governments in this Union repose excludes any general power of the state to standardize its children by forcing them to accept instruction from public teachers only. The child is not the mere creature of the state; those who nurture him and direct his destiny have the right coupled with the high duty to recognize and prepare him for additional obligations.*[13]

But despite all this, in a sense the question of public versus private schools was minor in the 1920s in the United States, for a second social movement ensured that the public school would not face substantial private competition—the nationalization of trade schools.

Trade schools were a Russian invention. When the Moscow Imperial Technical School (the first such school in the world) was founded in 1868, the institution at first only offered apprenticeships, but later added formal training classes modeled after those offered art and music students at the time. When these techniques were brought to America as part of the Russian exhibit at

7

the Centennial Exhibition in Philadelphia in 1876, they proved wildly popular with American educators. The first vocational school in America was created at Washington University in St. Louis in 1879; it was followed by manual-training schools in Cleveland, Cincinnati, and other cities. These schools offered quite extensive programs; historian Lawrence Cremin notes that the New York Trades School, founded in 1881, taught "bricklaying, plastering, plumbing, carpentry, stonecutting, blacksmithing, tailoring, and printing."[14] The New York Trades School had a substantial endowment; in 1892 J. P. Morgan gave the school a grant of $500,000.

In the first decade of the twentieth century, the trade school movement was well established. Such major corporations as Westinghouse and General Electric had established training and apprenticeship programs for their workers that lasted up to four years. In Chicago, Edwin Conley, the city's superintendent of schools between 1900 and 1909, proposed replacing America's system of public elementary schools with a national system of private vocational schools. His efforts were backed by the Chicago Commercial Club, the city's leading organization of businessmen.

Until 1905, the efforts of Chicago's reformers were endorsed by the National Association of Manufacturers (NAM). In a 1905 report, NAM stated that "trade schools properly protected from the domination and withering blight of organized labor are the one and only remedy for the present intolerable conditions" in American schools.[15] (During this period, NAM also favored increased immigration on the grounds that immigrants were less likely than native-born Americans to commit crimes, catch diseases, and accept charity during depressions.) But between 1905 and 1910, NAM's view shifted dramatically—a shift that ensured that for the rest of the century public schools would face little competition.

In 1906, the National Society for the Promotion of Industrial Education (NSPIE) was founded to lobby for vocational education. Their efforts quickly paid off. Within a year of its founding, President Theodore Roosevelt addressed the society's annual convention. President Roosevelt argued that America was engaged in a global struggle for "the markets of the world" that would be won by "the countries of greatest industrial efficiency." The best way to aid "the private soldiers of the national army," Roosevelt said, was by federal aid to vocational education.[16]

The NSPIE's Board of Directors included such prominent Americans as Jane Addams, Nicholas Murray Butler, and Frederick Winslow Taylor, all of whom wanted public schools to expand substantially. And the society produced reams of documents to support its case; by 1907 the State Superintendent of Schools in New Hampshire complained that "we are besieged with public documents, monographs, magazine articles, reports of investigations too numerous to mention, etc., etc.," all supporting state-funded industrial education.[17]

But all this paperwork paid off. By 1910, both big business and big labor found the NSPIE's case persuasive, primarily because each organization thought that government-funded industrial education would ensure that training programs would not be dominated by their rivals. The American Federation of Labor (AFL), reported historian Lawrence Cremin, supported nationalized vocational education because "the ineptness of the educators was less to be feared than the self-serving of the businessmen."[18]

A system of private trade schools, the AFL's industrial education committee charged in a 1910 report, would be "wholly removed from the salutary supervision of the people. . . . Any scheme of education which depends for its carrying out on a private group, subject to no public control, leaves unsolved the fundamental democratic problem of giving the boys of the country an equal opportunity and the citizens the power to criticize and reform the educational machinery."[19]

For its part, NAM backed government control of training programs for two reasons. State control, thought the manufacturers, would mean that labor unions could not use these training programs as recruiting grounds for new members. Second, notes Washington University historian Arthur G. Wirth, NAM's endorsement of tax-funded vocational education was part of the association's general endorsement of government subsidies to corporations. "When proposals were made to use federal taxes

9

for groups or interests outside the sphere of business," Wirth wrote, "the N.A.M. objected. But when the issue was the advancement of business welfare—with which the public welfare was equated—the manufacturers felt no hesitancy in appealing for federal action and financial support."[20]

At the time, NAM supported other government programs aiding business—federal regulation of railroad freight rates, building the Panama Canal, and subsidies to the merchant marine. Given this record, Wirth argues, NAM's "endorsement of federal support for industrial education was quite predictable."[21]

Thus by 1912 business and labor had united in support of government-controlled training programs. In that year, the NSPIE hired as its secretary Charles Allan Prosser, a dynamic lobbyist, who convinced President Woodrow Wilson to fund a national commission to study the need for vocational education. As the commission's members were all NSPIE members, everyone who testified—the representatives of the National Education Association, the General Federation of Women's Clubs, and so on—supported more federal aid to vocational education. Even the U.S. Army's representative, Capt. Douglas MacArthur, was enthusiastic about the program. Some were more than enthusiastic. When H. E. Miles, chairman of NAM's Committee on Industrial Education, was asked how much vocational education America needed, he answered, "an infinite amount. No man can measure it."[22]

When the Commission on National Aid to Vocational Education made its report, they made three arguments in favor of federally funded vocational education. First, they argued that the problem was too large to be handled by states or by the private sector. Second, they contended that U.S. productivity would be improved by having seven million young people acquire skills; this large work force was in the commission's eyes "an untrained army needing industrial education to make it efficient."[23] But the argument the commission considered most persuasive was that industrial education would allow American corporations to compete with foreign rivals. "The battles of the future between nations will be fought in the markets of the world," the commission predicted. "Our foreign commerce, and to some extent our domestic commerce, are being threatened by the commercial prestige which Germany has won, largely as the result of a policy of training its workers begun by the far-seeing Bismarck almost half-a-century ago."[24]

Such arguments proved persuasive with Congress, which in 1917 passed the Smith-Hughes Act authorizing federal funds for vocational education. The passage of the act had two consequences. First, Smith-Hughes was the first major federal education program; until that time, the federal government's role in American education was to hold conferences and collect statistics, not subsidize schools directly. Second, the industrial education movement ensured that public schools would dominate the American education system. Private schools provided an alternative for the few students whose parents could afford tuition, but the millions of high school students who were not able or willing to go to college now had two options—take public school shop classes or drop out. So by 1920 the structure of American education was set in place.

The education debate shifted from whether public or private schools would dominate to what was taught in public schools. For the first half of the century, educators argued over the nature and extent of "progressive" or "child-centered" education. "Progressive education" is used for two movements, one of which succeeded the other. The first movement, which lasted from 1890 and 1910, changed the way American schools were organized and controlled. The second wave of progressive educators, who flourished between 1915 and 1955, altered school curricula dramatically.

The Progressives who transformed American high schools from isolated ones controlled by local school boards to larger, more homogenous, less democratic districts did so for three reasons. First, the Progressives felt that control of schools should be as far up the bureaucratic ladder as possible. In 1890, for example, most high schools in America's larger cities were controlled by "ward boards," which controlled most of the ordinary functions of hiring, firing, and buying in high schools. In Pittsburgh, for example, ward boards hired teachers, determined the property tax rate, built new schools, and maintained old ones; the city school board could only hire principals and buy textbooks. Because there could be as many as a dozen ward boards in a larger city, schools tended to be run either by parents or people of the same class and background as those who attended the schools.

The Progressives successfully abolished ward boards, drastically reduced the size of school boards, and placed as much power in the hands of the school superintendent as possible. These reformers tended to be wealthy WASPs fearful both of immigrants and of democracy. Thus Edward Page, a prominent Progressive in New York City, warned Mayor William Strong in 1896 that ward boards should not continue; it was not wise in a city like this, so impregnated with foreign influence, that the school should be controlled locally, for in many localities the influence that would control would be unquestionably un-American. "In some districts, there are vast throngs of foreigners where one scarcely hears a word of English spoken, where the mode of living is repugnant to every American."[25]

The Progressives successfully led the effort to abolish ward boards and reduce school board size. In 1893, the 28 cities in the U.S. with populations of over 100,000 had between them 603 elected members of school boards as well as hundreds more elected to ward boards; by 1913 these cities had only 264 school board members and ward boards had been abolished. Not until the late 1980s would the ward board be revived as a "parent council" or as "school-based management."

Allied to this notion was the theory that a properly trained administrator could be as competent in Portland, Oregon, as in Portland, Maine, thus ensuring that schools would be increasingly governed by "experts" unfamiliar with the personalities and conflicts of a given area. By moving power high up the bureaucratic ladder, parents, teachers, and principals increasingly became middle managers, not those in charge of the system. The "reforms" of the Progressives ended up harming public schools for nearly a century.

If the first generation of Progressives worked to alter the way schools were run, the second generation of Progressives strived to change what was taught in the public schools. The birth of "progressive education" in America can not be dated with precision. The first progressive school, the Laboratory School of the University of Chicago, was created by John Dewey in 1896. But although advocates of curricular change agitated for years, their triumph was delayed until after World War I, partly due to the intellectual exhaustion that plagued America during this period.

Three events between 1916 and 1920 ensured the dominance of progressive education in American high schools. In 1916, John Dewey published *Democracy and Education,* an impenetrable treatise that liberal education reformers of the 1920s revered as fervently as their successors in the 1960s worshipped the works of Jonathan Kozol, Paul Goodman, or John Holt. In 1918, William Heard Kilpatrick, Dewey's leading disciple, began his career at Columbia University's Teachers College. Kilpatrick reportedly trained more teachers than anyone else in America (he is said to have taught 35,000 students over his lengthy career), and most students left Kilpatrick's courses agreeing with his central thesis: The traditional subjects of American high schools should be replaced with curricula that respond to the student's "felt needs." "The true unit of study," Kilpatrick noted in a 1936 article, was not reading, writing, or arithmetic but the "organism-in-its-interaction-with-the-environment."[26]

But the key document of American progressive education was a report, *Cardinal Principles of Secondary Education,* published by the U.S. Office of Education in 1918. Like *A Nation at Risk* some 65 years later, *Cardinal Principles* was the final report of a national commission; and in clear, precise, and strident English, it called for dramatic reforms. (Unlike *A Nation at Risk,* however, *Cardinal Principles* was prepared by the National Education Association, which had moved to Washington the year before to influence education policy nationally.)

There were seven "Cardinal Principles" of education, with such titles as "Worthy Home-Membership" and "Worthy Use of Leisure-Time." Only one of the seven principles stressed the importance of learning traditional subjects; the remainder emphasized, over and over and over again, that the purpose of

American education was not to teach students skills but to prepare students for "life." The fundamental purpose of American high schools, said *Cardinal Principles*, was to teach a pupil to "find his place" in a democracy "and use that place to shape both himself and society towards ever nobler ends." Subjects, the report added, should be designed to advance collectivist goals; civics, for example, "should help to establish a genuine internationalism, free from sentimentality, founded on fact, and actually operative in the affairs of nations."[27]

Some reforms first advocated by *Cardinal Principles* are common practice today. It was the first major report to advocate the division of junior and senior high schools as well as allowing students to choose some classes through electives. But it was the theories espoused by *Cardinal Principles* not the practice that made the report influential in the 1920s and 1930s. By 1929, 110,000 copies of the report had been sold, an amazing number for a government report, then or now. Indeed, according to historian Samuel Blumenfeld, some teacher training colleges insisted on their students memorizing the Cardinal Principles as part of their studies.[28]

In the 1920s, thanks to *Cardinal Principles*, teacher training colleges, and journals of education, the ideas of progressive education dominated American life. From Maine to Texas, Oregon to Florida, these progressive educators insisted on implementing "life education" classes, "common learnings," or other courses which had little to do with education's traditional themes. By the mid-1930s, notes historian Diane Ravitch, 70 percent of cities with populations of over 25,000 had set up curriculum-revising committees; half of the towns with populations between 5,000 and 25,000 had established similar organizations.[29]

Unlike the changes in American high schools that had taken place in the past, the progressive education movement was an attempt to implement changes nationally. Since the turn of the century, there had been an informal national curriculum in America; each year, the College Board published a list of courses it believed high school students should take to prepare for further education. In 1901, for example, the board's list included works by Shakespeare and Longfellow. But the College Board's proposals were merely suggestions that did not have the force of law.

The progressive educators wanted their ideas and changes to prevail everywhere. As Diane Ravitch perceptively notes:

> *Whether the community was rural, suburban, or urban, whether the local economy was based on farming, mining or trade, whether the children came from wealth or poverty, the curriculum revisions echoed the language of the progressive textbooks.*[30]

Thus all across America, reformers told school boards that "the total life activity" of the child mattered more than what was taught, and that grading was purely mechanistic and did not reflect what the student actually learned. And school boards responded. Attendance in college preparatory classes fell, and some school systems implemented drastic changes. In Ann Arbor, Michigan, for example, the school board voted to ban all textbooks. Three years later, the board allowed the reintroduction of spelling books, to the great relief of Ann Arbor teachers.

In the 1920s, as part of the high school's transformation from a temple of learning to a leisure-time palace, social clubs began to flourish. A survey conducted by the Massachusetts Department of Education in 1928 found clubs devoted to cameras, radio, salesmanship, guns, etiquette, aircraft, ethics, prohibitionism, ukelele, banjo, and poultry. Dress codes also date from this period, usually created by students as a means of peer pressure. The students in Madison, Wisconsin's high school, for example, voted in 1922 to prohibit short skirts, loud talking, and "undue familiarity with boys."

By the 1930s, progressive education was the dominant educational philosophy in high schools. But some disciples of Dewey proposed even more radical reforms. In *Dare the School Build a New Social Order?* (1932), George S. Counts, a colleague of Dewey's at Teachers College, Columbia University, called on high school teachers to strive for collectivism, to "repress every form of privilege and economic parasitism," and to implement revolution. "That the teachers should deliberately reach for power and then make the most of their conquest is my firm conviction," Counts wrote.[31]

Dewey, for his part, thought that his disciples had become too rigid; in *Experience and Education* (1938), Dewey warned that "an educational philosophy which professes to be based on the idea of freedom may become as dogmatic as ever was the traditional education which it reacted against."[32] By 1950 Dewey's warning had proven prophetic. Progressive education was the received wisdom of the day; "life-adjustment education" was the vanguard of educational thought. But the critics of progressivism were gaining ground. Led by University of Chicago president Robert Maynard Hutchins, philosopher Mortimer Adler, University of Illinois scholar Arthur Bestor, and Admiral Hyman Rickover, the "back to basics" critics of progressive education launched a steady barrage of books, articles, and critiques, and formed the Council on Basic Education in 1955. Journalists added to the ridicule of the regnant Progressives; in a 1951 article, for example, one critic said that "life-adjustment education" meant that teachers were little more than "umpires in the battle of the vertical versus the horizontal in tooth-brushing."[33]

The launch of *Sputnik* in 1957 marked the end of U.S. prominence over the Soviet Union in science, and the end of the reign of progressive education in American high schools. *Sputnik*, to many American educators, meant an end to frills and follies in the high school; new federal programs authorized under the National Defense Education Act meant millions for schools to teach additional courses in math and science to close the gap between U.S. and Soviet expertise.

But the triumph of the traditionalists was Pyrrhic. In the long run, the Progressives had won because they had undermined the authority of principals and teachers over students. Syracuse University education professor Gerald Grant explains this loss of authority by comparing high schools to various kinds of fruit.[34] In 1900 Grant sees the American high school as being like an avocado—fairly small, with a solid center of authority and a "skin of external policy, thin and well-defined." By 1950, the progressive educators had turned the high school into a cantaloupe-like organization: larger, with a hollow core but with a relatively firm skin of rules and command. Today, according to Grant, the American high school is like a watermelon, with a thick rind of regulations, no well-defined center, and teachers scattered like watermelon seeds, uncertain what they can and cannot do.

Another lasting legacy of progressive education is the trend to consolidate school districts and school boards. In 1900, there were 100,000 school districts in America; by 1985, there were fewer than 20,000.[35] With each closing of a school board, decisions were made about students that were farther and farther removed from principals and teachers. While the trend toward school consolidation was instituted and sanctioned by the progressive educators, it increased in the 1960s and 1970s as a result of massive increases in federal aid to education.

Huge increases in the federal education budget were first proposed during the Truman Administration. In 1946 and 1947, the large number of returning veterans flooding schools on the G.I. Bill prompted many of the mandarins of education journalism to declare that public schools were in a "crisis" that could only be resolved by boosts in the federal education budget. Benjamin Fine, education editor of the *New York Times* at the time, declared that America was "spending less of its national income on schools than either Great Britain or the Soviet Union."

The endless cries of doom gave the advocates of greater education spending an opportunity to create a national department of education. In 1948, Sen. Robert Taft (R-Ohio), the leading American conservative politician of the era, switched sides and declared his support for greater federal education spending, declaring that children "were entitled as a matter of right to a decent place in which to go to school."

"Education is socialistic anyway," Senator Taft added, "and has been for a hundred and fifty years."[36]

Senator Taft introduced a bill that would grant states federal funds amounting to five dollars per student, allowing the states to decide whether these funds would go to parochial schools. The bill also explicitly barred federal interference in education.

Senator Taft's bill passed the Senate twice in 1948 and 1949. But in the House, Rep. Graham Burden (D-North Carolina), chairman of the House Education and Labor Committee, refused to allow any bill that would give federal funds to parochial schools to be considered by his committee. Representative Burden's firm opposition to parochial school aid convinced Catholics, particularly Cardinal Spellman, to mount an all-out effort to block any federal aid to education package from passing Congress. The unyielding opposition of Burden and the relentless lobbying by Catholics delayed federal aid to education for nearly 20 years.

In 1958, during the Eisenhower Administration, the National Defense Education Act was passed; it provided nearly $1 billion (out of a total federal budget of $74 billion) for programs in math and science. The ensuing Kennedy Administration, Democratic and liberal, was elected by a paper-thin majority; President Kennedy was far more concerned with foreign policy than with domestic issues, and no new federal education programs were instituted.

The crushing defeat Lyndon Johnson gave Barry Goldwater in 1964 ensured vast growth in federal education spending. Johnson had graduated from a teachers college and had briefly taught classes himself. While most of the Great Society welfare programs were not channeled for education, the passage of the Elementary and Secondary Education Act in 1965 ensured increases in federal education spending of over $1.5 billion a year, chiefly through a program known as "Title I" that provided federal aid to students with incomes below the poverty line. The Head Start program, instituted in 1964, was another federal education budget-booster.

The Nixon Administration's policy toward federal education spending was similar to its attitude toward welfare spending in general. No new programs were added; none was cancelled. During the Nixon years, however, the Office of Economic Opportunity (OEO) conducted the first—and, until the late 1980s, the last—experiment in public school choice.

In 1970, the OEO tried to find a school district that would consider a voucher test. Superintendents in several large districts (most notably the state of New Hampshire and the city of East Hartford, Connecticut) attempted to apply for OEO funds, but union pressure resulted in these districts withdrawing from the

18

proposed plan. Only in Alum Rock, California (a suburb of San Jose), did a school district volunteer for a voucher program.[37]

Between 1971 and 1974, the 7,500 students in Alum Rock were able to move between schools in the district. Surveys were regularly taken of parents to judge their satisfaction with the program. In 1974, the Alum Rock experiment concluded. By the 1973/74 year, only 15 percent of the parents had moved their children from one school to another; surveys had shown modest increases in parent satisfaction as well as a small rise in support for schools in general.[38]

But the Alum Rock experiment was a limited one. Parents could not choose high schools; nor could they use the money spent on public schools for private schools. (Although the Alum Rock experiment has often been described as a voucher program, it was a program of public school choice rather than a fully transferable voucher since there were no private schools in the district.) Teacher tenure was assured, moreover, removing a key test of competition between schools. Thus the Alum Rock experiment was inconclusive; what makes it significant is that no other attempt at public school choice was tried for more than 15 years.

In the 1970s, federal education spending grew steadily, rising from $4.5 billion in 1966 to $13.4 billion in 1974 and to $19.5 billion in 1978 (roughly its current level, adjusted for inflation). But despite or, perhaps, because of these huge increases in education spending, public schools became increasingly less effective. Average scores on the Scholastic Aptitude Test (SAT) steadily fell, dropping from an average of 463 in 1966 to 429 in 1978.[39] The intellectual rebellions of the 1960s were replaced by thuggery and violence; a 1978 report from the National Institute of Education noted that 2.4 million thefts occurred in schools each month and that two-thirds of inner-city high schools had security guards.

The 1970s also marked the high point of the political power of the two national teachers' unions. Both the National Education Association (NEA), which traced its roots to an organization created in 1857, and the American Federation of Teachers (AFT) had existed for a long time. Although the AFT in its current form was created in 1960, the United Federation of Teachers—the New

19

York City teachers' union, which is the largest component of the AFT—was created in 1916. (The holder of United Federation of Teachers card no. 1 was John Dewey.)

Until the 1970s, the NEA had thought of itself as a professional organization rather than a union; until 1976, for example, the NEA refused to endorse a presidential candidate. Until 1968, moreover, the NEA had insisted that its members not strike. When a committee of the NEA in 1960 suggested that the association adopt as its theme for the coming year "Every Teacher a Politician," it was rejected because few in the NEA thought of themselves as political. While the AFT and its predecessors did see themselves as unions (and were, in fact, founded so that teachers might be represented in the AFL and its successors), the AFT had always been much smaller than the NEA and had had proportionally less influence nationally.

But by the 1970s both of the teachers' unions began to lobby for more federal funds for education as well as for more perks for their members. NEA lobbyists, in fact, had helped ensure passage of Great Society education programs. (In the late 1960s and early 1970s the AFT had steadily gained ground over its rival, winning several locals that had formerly belonged to the NEA.) By 1972, the National Education Association had become radicalized. In that year, school administrators left the organization; only then did the NEA become a *teachers' union*, not a national association of educators. Not only did NEA leaders see themselves as a union but they realized that they were the only union with members in every congressional district. Although the NEA could do little to help George McGovern from his crushing defeat by Richard Nixon, NEA leaders loudly proclaimed their support for radical reforms. In 1956, only one-quarter of the NEA members surveyed said that teachers should participate in politics; by 1975, 92.6 percent of the delegates to the NEA convention agreed with the union's decision to endorse a presidential candidate.

In 1976 the NEA did its part to help Jimmy Carter narrowly defeat Gerald Ford. The NEA endorsed Carter, and teacher lobbyists ensured victory for Carter in several states, notably Pennsylvania, Ohio, and Florida. Because Carter's margin of

20

victory was very narrow (in the electoral college, it was the lowest since Woodrow Wilson in 1916), NEA support was more crucial than would have been the case in a more decisive election.

As reward for the education union's efforts, President Carter fulfilled one of his campaign pledges and began to press for creation of a separate Department of Education. Aside from the NEA, few people were in favor of such a department. The editorial pages of the *New York Times, Washington Post, Chicago Tribune*, and the *Wall Street Journal* were all opposed, as was the American Federation of Teachers. NEA and Carter Administration support nonetheless ensured that a bill creating the department would pass the House of Representatives by a 14-vote margin in 1978 (the margin in the Senate was slightly higher).

Fresh from creating their own Cabinet department, National Education Association leaders prepared for greater triumphs. Few organizations have had the power to create their own federal government department, but in hindsight creation of the Department of Education marked the limits of NEA power. In 1980, the NEA once again threw its organizational support to Jimmy Carter, ignoring the NEA members (up to one-third by some accounts) who were registered Republicans. (The AFT only supported Carter after their preferred candidate, Sen. Edward Kennedy [D—Massachusetts] dropped out of the race.) But despite the efforts of 500,000 NEA volunteers, Carter's defeat ensured the end of NEA influence in the department it had created. In 1984, the NEA proved to be one of the few unions staunchly supporting Walter Mondale; the second defeat of an NEA-backed presidential candidate put the union further on the defensive.

During the Reagan Administration, the war between conservatives and liberals over the nature and purpose of federal education spending ended in a stalemate. Although one of Ronald Reagan's campaign promises was abolition of the Department of Education, the action was never seriously considered. As in the debates over federal welfare spending, liberals had the power to preserve existing programs, even when they were ineffectual. A 1989 report from the General Accounting Office, for example, showed that the Department of Education had no idea whether the billions spent on Chapter 1 (the renamed Title I) funds in fact went to poor people.

But while few of the Department of Education's programs were cut, few programs were added. The Department of Education in 1990 was little changed from what it had been in 1980. A few onerous regulations, chiefly in the area of bilingual education, had been rescinded, and Secretary of Education William Bennett (1985–1988) had made useful comments about the nature and purpose of education.

But with the Department of Education preserved as if in amber, the changes taking place in education were the result of state and local, not federal, initiatives. These changes—more choice by parents in schooling, greater control of schools by teachers, a restoration of authority by principals, and a return of morality to the schools—are the subjects of subsequent chapters.

NOTES

1. Lloyd Jorgenson, *The State and the Non-Public School, 1825–1925* (Lexington: University Press of Kentucky, 1987), p. 37 ff.
2. Lawrence Cremin, *American Education: The National Experience* (New York: Harper & Row, 1980), p. 176.
3. Cited in Cremin, op. cit., p. 95.
4. Cited in Jorgenson, op. cit., p. 27.
5. Ibid., p. 38.
6. Ibid., p. 83. See also Vincent P. Lannie and Bernard C. Diethorn, "For the Honor and Glory of God: The Philadelphia Bible Riots of 1840," *History of Education Quarterly*, Spring 1968.
7. Charles Glenn, *Choice of Schools in Six Nations* (Washington, D.C.: U.S. Department of Education, 1989), p. 52.
8. *Religion and Society Report*, May 1990.
9. The most informative article on these attempted Catholic-state school mergers is Marvin Lazerson, "Understanding American Catholic Educational History," *History of Education Quarterly*, Fall 1977.
10. Jorgenson, op. cit., p. 138.
11. David Tyack, "The Perils of Pluralism: The Background of the Pierce Case," *American Historical Review*, October 1968.
12. Jorgenson, op. cit., p. 209.
13. Ibid., p. 210.
14. Ibid., pp. 224–225.
15. Lawrence Cremin, *The Transformation of the School: Progressivism in American Education, 1876–1907* (New York: Alfred A. Knopf, 1961), p. 37.
16. Ibid., p. 38.
17. Arthur G. Wirth, *The Vocational-Liberal Studies Controversy Between John Dewey and Others (1900–1917)* (Washington, D.C.: U.S. Office of Education, 1970), p. 39.
18. Cremin, *Transformation*, p. 116.
19. Ibid., p. 38.
20. Wirth, op. cit., p. 56.
21. Ibid.
22. *Vocational Education: Report of the Commission on National Aid to Vocational Education* (Washington, D.C.: Government Printing Office, 1914), v. 2, p. 270.
23. Ibid., v. 1, p. 21.

24. Ibid., v. 1, p. 24.
25. David Tyack, *The One Best System* (Cambridge, MA: Harvard University Press, 1974), p. 89.
26. Cited in Diane Ravitch, *The Troubled Crusade: American Education, 1945–1980* (New York: Basic Books, 1983), p. 58.
27. *Cardinal Principles of Secondary Education* (Washington, D.C.: Bureau of Education, 1918), p. 19.
28. Samuel L. Blumenfeld, *NEA: Trojan Horse in American Education* (Boise, ID: Paradigm, 1984), p. 66.
29. Ravitch, op. cit., p. 56.
30. Ibid., p. 53.
31. George S. Counts, *Dare the School Build a New Social Order?* (New York: John Day, 1932), p. 41.
32. Cited in Ravitch, op. cit., p. 59. *Experience and Education* was published in 1938.
33. Ibid., p. 73. The article was originally published in *Scientific Monthly* in 1951.
34. Gerald Grant, *What We Learned at Hamilton High* (Cambridge, MA: Harvard University Press, 1988), pp. 124–125.
35. Lawrence Uzzell, *Contradictions of Centralized Education* (Washington, D.C.: Cato Institute, 1985), p. 1.
36. Ravitch, op. cit., p. 17.
37. David K. Cohen and Eleanor Farrar, "Power to the Parents?—The Story of Education Vouchers," *Public Interest*, Summer 1977.
38. Ibid. See also John Coons and Stephen D. Sugarman, *Education by Choice: The Case for Family Control* (Berkeley, CA: University of California Press, 1978).
39. Uzzell, op. cit., p. 2.

2

TEACHING VALUES IN SCHOOLS

We think it ordinary to spend twelve or sixteen or twenty years of a person's life and many thousands of public dollars on 'education'—and not a dime or a thought on character. Of course, it is preposterous to suppose that character could be cultivated by any sort of public program. Persons of character are not public products. They are made by local cultures, local responsibilities.[1]

Wendell Berry

Education is not to teach men what they do not know, but to teach men to behave as they do not behave.[2]

John Ruskin

Wisdom and knowledge, as well as virtue, diffused generally among the body of the people, being necessary for the preservation of their rights and liberties ... it shall be the duty of Legislatures and Magistrates ... [and] public and grammar schools in the towns ... to countenance and inculcate the principles of humanity and general benevolence, public and private charity, industry and frugality, honesty and punctuality in their dealings with society, good humour, and all social affections, and generous sentiments among the people.[3]

Constitution of the State of Massachusetts (1780)

A rising number of parents, teachers, and scholars are demanding that schools teach their children values. In a recent Gallup poll, 84 percent of public school parents surveyed declared that they wanted "moral values" taught in school, and 68 percent wanted schools to develop standards of right and wrong.[4] In June 1990, the National Council of Catholic Bishops and the Synagogue Council of America (representing the three branches of Judaism) issued a statement urging all public schools to teach morality as part of their curriculum. Such qualities as "honesty, compassion, integrity, tolerance, loyalty, and belief in human worth and dignity," noted the bishops and rabbis, "are embedded in our respective religious traditions and in the civic fabric of our society."[5]

Politicians have also increased their calls for teaching values in the schools. While formerly many of the politicians who attacked "value-free" curriculums were conservatives, today such prominent liberals as New York Governor Mario Cuomo, former California Superintendent of Schools William Honig, and People for the American Way president John H. Buchanan, Jr., have come out for restoring morality to the classroom.

In 1990, aided by a $21 million grant from Laurance Rockefeller, Princeton University established a Center for Human Values to study, among other issues, how and why schools should teach morality. "It is important that both the educational system and parents inculcate virtue," says the center's director, political philosopher Amy Gutmann. "Neither parents nor the educational system should offer children the choice as to whether to be honest or not."[6] Congress is also paying attention; a bill introduced by Representative Tony Hall (D-Ohio) would create a national commission to study when and how such principles as honesty, tolerance, and love of country should be taught in the classroom. "I fear that our nation is plunging into a national moral recession,"[7] Congressman Hall said. But teaching values is not as simple as teaching reading or arithmetic. Which values, for example, should be taught? How should they be taught? And can teaching alone ensure that students become worthy citizens? These are not simple issues. In fact, they are among the perennial questions of philosophy.

The first critic of what is now called "character education" was Aristotle. In the *Nicomachean Ethics*, Aristotle taught that teaching "political science" (what would now be called civics and ethics) to young people would be "vain and unprofitable," as the young are both too passionate and too inexperienced in the ways of the world.[8]

But by the nineteenth century, doubts about teaching virtue in the classroom had dissipated. Until the First World War, the consensus among American educators was that teaching morality was as natural as teaching writing or arithmetic. As historian Ruth Miller Elson observes, one of the primary purposes of nineteenth century textbooks was to teach children virtue by describing the lives of such American heroes as Benjamin Franklin, George Washington, and Abraham Lincoln. For example, Charles Augustus Goodrich's *A History of the United States of America* (which went through 150 editions between 1823 and 1873) states in its preface that one of its purposes was to present "striking instances of virtue, enterprise, courage, generosity, patriotism, and, by a principle of emulation, incite us to copy such noble examples.[9]

Nineteenth century educators also believed that the Bible should be the teacher's inseparable companion. In 1869, for example, the National Teachers Association (the predecessor of the National Education Association) issued a resolution that "the Bible should not only be studied, venerated, and honored as a classic for all ages, peoples, and languages, but devotionally read, and its precepts inculcated in all the common schools of the land."[10]

But from 1885 onwards, the Bible-based curriculum began to be replaced. Newly minted doctors of education increasingly believed that the moral principles contained in the Bible could be scientifically extracted and presented in a way that did not imply approval of any religion. "There is a secular morality which is not opposed to religious morality," noted an article that appeared in the *Wisconsin Journal of Education* in the 1880s, that "is recognized by all civilized people, is taught by the philosophers of all nations, and is sanctioned by all religious creeds."[11]

By the 1920s, educators thought that universally applicable

moral courses could be taught through what became known as "character education." The movement began with the creation in 1911 of the Character Education Institution, which later changed its name to the National Institution for Moral Education. Armed with the newly created social science tools of statistical analysis, character educators believed that the behavior of children could be quantified as precisely as the movement of atoms. The National Institution for Moral Education, for example, determined that there were precisely ninety-one forms of virtue and six types of character (intellectual, working, personal, social, emotional, and physical). A competitor in turn created the Utah Plan, which was based on "the law of ideo-meter action." This was that "every idea which gains lodgment in the mind tends to express itself in action." As historian Stephen Yulish noted, "stripped of its social science veneer, the Utah Plan largely consisted of memorizing poetry, proverbs, and 'beautiful uplifting sayings.'"[12]

Before the decade ended, schools across America were implementing character education. National organizations such as Uncle Sam's Boys and Girls gave children medals and badges for good conduct. In Chicago in 1931, there were more than 200 competing character education plans schools could adopt.

Despite this success, in the early 1930s character education began to decline. This was largely due to the Character Education Inquiry, a team of researchers at Teachers College at Columbia University that spent 5 years examining character education in the late 1920s. In a three-volume report, the inquiry concluded that the character education movement was at best ineffective and occasionally caused students to become more immoral by cheating on good conduct records. The reason: outside influences on students' lives equalled or exceeded school influence. For example, students who attended movies more than once a week were more likely to commit immoral deeds than students who went to movies less frequently.

"Learning of self-control, as also of service and honesty, is largely a matter of accident," the inquiry concluded. "Peculiarities of home, church, school, Sunday school, teacher, club leader,

28

and everything else that deliberately attempts to influence the child work upon him by divers means and with divers result."[13]

Although character education left some imprint on the American classroom for the next 35 years (such as the creation of homerooms and student governments), teaching values lost ground among American educators. Not until the 1960s did moral education again become a tool to mold the hearts and minds of students.

Two competing schools of moral education emerged in the 1960s: the "values clarification" movement, led by Sidney Simon, an education professor at the University of Massachusetts; and the "just community" scholars, disciples of Lawrence Kohlberg, a psychologist at Harvard University.

The values clarifiers derived their principles from Carl Rogers (1902–1987), one of the more important American psychologists of the twentieth century. Rogers was the founder of what became known as "client-centered" or "nondirective" therapy. Human beings, Rogers thought, were inherently good, but their goodness was blocked by being forced into roles not of their choosing. The therapist's job was to try to direct the client to discover his own values by intensive discussions in what became known as "encounter groups" or "T-groups." In these groups, the therapist acted as a leader to keep the discussion flowing. A primary goal of the Rogerians was that the therapist not tell the clients what to think or what values were proper or just; the goal was for the client to discover his or her meaning or purpose and become a whole, complete, and "self-actualized" person. This notion of Rogers—that one should not impose values on someone else—eventually became a commonplace.

Rogers had a longstanding interest in education, and in 1967 he published a paper calling for a school system willing to try out his theories. Rogers thought if the majority of people in a school went through encounter group therapy, people would stop seeing each other as roles or job descriptions and begin to see each other as human beings. Instead of seeing a boss or a colleague as a superintendent, school board member, or supervisor, Rogers wrote, people in schools would "begin to interact

29

as persons, whole persons with feelings as well as thoughts, capable of being hurt as well as being actualized."[14]

Rogers believed that if his theories were put into practice, artificial hierarchies would break down and students would begin to enjoy learning instead of thinking of studying as a painful chore. But Rogers did not think his theories would work unless most of the people in a school system went to encounter groups. Encounter group therapy, said Rogers, "cannot be used in the most effective manner unless the *whole system* is moving towards changingness in a way which accommodates change in its own units.[15] "This plan could result in the kind of educational revolution which is needed to bring about the confidence in the *process* of learning, the *process* of change, rather than static knowledge." Rogers concluded. "ANY TAKERS?"[16]

The Sisters of the Immaculate Heart of Mary, a Catholic order located in Los Angeles, agreed. In 1968 the nuns agreed to operate its 59 schools along Rogerian lines. Most of the nuns entered the process of self-actualization with gusto. "I have been able to confess anxiety to my classes, and consequently feel more comfortable than I ever felt before," one teacher at Immaculate Heart College wrote in her journal. "I am not giving grades, and am not even giving exams. They are writing their own questions—the ones that are meaningful to them in terms of the material, and then discussing them."[17]

But the nuns were so eager to practice self-actualization, so compelled by what they learned in their encounter groups, that they no longer thought of themselves as Catholics. The nuns, wrote William R. Coulson, a project coordinator of the Immaculate Heart experiment, "had asked themselves as an organization the same question which they learned can make an encounter group prosper: 'Are we doing what we want to do?' Are we doing what we want to do when Cardinal McIntyre tells us when to get up in the morning and what clothes to wear and how to say our prayers? When their answer was a near-unanimous 'No,' they stopped doing it, and then the Cardinal didn't want them teaching in his schools."[18] After self-actualization, the Sisters of the Immaculate Heart of Mary declared that they were no longer nuns and withdrew from the Catholic church. The church cut off funds to the Immaculate Heart schools.

In 1968 the sisters operated 59 schools with 600 nuns; by 1972, there were two schools and no nuns. By 1980, even these two schools closed their doors.

The "values clarifiers" were Rogerians, but their goals were more limited than Rogers himself wanted; there were no attempts to have teachers and administrators clarify their values. But the values clarifiers took as their first principle the Rogerian notion that teachers should not attempt to decide what students' values were. Rather than trying to teach morality, Simon and his colleagues argued, what schools should do was persuade students to discover their own values. "People have to prize for themselves, choose for themselves, integrate choices into the pattern of their own lives," Simon and his collaborators wrote in *Values and Teaching*, the seminal work of the values clarification movement. By working to clarify values, said Simon and his colleagues, the teacher "avoids moralizing, preaching, indoctrinating, inculcating, or dogmatizing."[20]

The values clarifier, Simon and his colleagues said, should not only urge his students to question authority but everything else as well. Through such arcane techniques as "one-legged conferences" and "rank-order" quizzes ("Who would be the easiest to live without: your parents, your friends, or your brothers and sisters?"[21]) the values clarifiers hoped to ensure that students discovered their values. Constant student quizzing was also of crucial importance. Here is a sample from *Values and Teaching*.

STUDENT: "It's not good to be lazy, you know."

TEACHER: "How do you know it's not good?"

STUDENT: "Everybody knows that. My parents
          always say it."

TEACHER: (walking away) "I see."[22]

Such methods may seem somewhat quaint today, but in the 1960s and 1970s they were wildly popular. Over 500,000 copies of Simon's textbooks were sold, and by 1975 ten state school boards recommended that values clarification be taught in their state's classrooms.

But by the late 1970s, values clarification was also in retreat. Parents increasingly worried that the method was teaching immorality; if whatever the value a student freely chose was "correct," what happened when a student, acting of his own free will, decided to become a violent criminal? Cries from the values clarifiers that this would never happen were unconvincing; values clarification could not produce a Hitler, one training manual noted, because "Hitler was clearly paranoid and could not effectively use the choosing process of valuing."[23]

By the 1980s, educational evaluators had studied values clarification and rendered their verdict: While values clarification did not harm students, neither did it help them. In 1978, for example, Alan Lockwood of the University of Wisconsin (Madison) examined thirteen studies of values clarification and concluded that twelve of them had "unwarranted statistical manipulations and interpretations" that called the findings of these studies into question. "Based on these studies," Lockwood reported, "there is no evidence that values clarification has a systematic, demonstrated impact on students' values."[24] Lockwood's conclusions were seconded by a 1988 Department of Education report noting numerous studies that "consistently conclude that, according to all the measures considered, values clarification does not appear to have any effect at all [on young people]."[25]

Competing with the values clarifiers was a school of educational psychologists known as either the "moral dilemma" or the "just community" school. These psychologists clustered around Lawrence Kohlberg (1927–1987), a Harvard psychologist. Kohlberg's name is little known outside educational circles, but he was probably the most influential educational theorist since John Dewey. Kohlberg saw himself as being in the sensible middle ground between the anarchy of the values clarifiers and the rigidity of traditional moral teaching. If the values clarifiers were heirs to the Romantics and to Rousseau, Kohlberg was a cool rationalist, a man of the Enlightenment and an intellectual descendant of Immanuel Kant.

In the 1950s, Kohlberg conducted a series of experiments to determine how young people learn about values. He quizzed hundreds of young people at various intervals during the decade, presenting them with a series of moral dilemmas. In his most famous case, he presented teenagers with the study of Heinz, whose wife was dying of cancer and needed a radium-based drug worth $2,000. Heinz, however, could only borrow $1,000 from the bank. Should he steal the drug?

Based on his research, Kohlberg concluded that everyone passes through precisely six stages of morality in the course of their lives. In the first stage, people believed that might was right; thus one subject, "Tommy," at age ten, said that Heinz shouldn't steal the drug because the government considered it theft. But by careful reflection and effective teaching, Kohlberg argued, people attained "stage six," wherein they would act like Nietzschean supermen, guiding their lives according to such abstract codes as the Golden Rule and the categorical imperative. Thus Tommy, at age sixteen, having attained stage six, argued that Heinz should steal the drug because "you can't put a price on love; you can't put a price on life."

"The reaching of virtue is the asking of questions and the pointing of the way," Kohlberg wrote in 1980, "not the giving of answers.... Moral education is the leading of men upward, not the putting into the mind of knowledge what was not there before."[26]

Kohlberg's views have been the subject of passionate debate among educational psychologists. Some of his critics argue that he reached his conclusions from too small a sample. Others believe that students trained by Kohlbergian methods do not necessarily change their behavior; they simply have more sophisticated justifications for their actions. But perhaps the most telling evidence concerning Kohlberg's theories lies in the attempts Kohlberg made to create a school that would fully reflect his principles.

In 1974 in the wake of Watergate, Kohlberg and his colleagues at Harvard's Center for Moral Education persuaded the city of Cambridge, Massachusetts, to allow them to oversee a public high school for a few years. The school was designed as a democratic institution; every decision the school made had to be ratified by an assembly comprised of students, teachers, and staff. But the high school refused to crystallize as a modern *polis.*

Few students attended the assemblies, and those who did considered them boring and ineffective. The only debates that aroused the student body as a whole were over whether or not to fly a Palestinian Liberation Organization flag in front of the school and whether or not drugs could be consumed in the hallways, and if so, which drugs could be used. (The content and nature of the curriculum was apparently never discussed.)

In his final book, published after his death, Kohlberg admitted that his grand experiment did not work; permissiveness did not result in morality. "The 1970s may be remembered as the decade of failed educational experimentation," Kohlberg wrote. "Open campuses, unstructured time and free schools lessened the restrictions on adolescents but did not directly foster self-direction or participation."[27]

Carl Rogers also reconsidered his views in the wake of the Immaculate Heart debacle. In a 1977 article in *Education Leadership,* Rogers warned that his ideas were not for everyone and that Rogerian "true believers" might well shut their minds to alternative ways of teaching. He also stated that schools should retain a place for teachers and students who wished to follow traditional moral standards. "How can we make sure that there is always a place for both students and faculty who desire a traditional education?" Rogers wrote. "We don't want to coerce people into freedom."[28]

In his last book, *Freedom to Learn for the '80s* (1983), Rogers revised his views further. Rogers never abandoned his core principle that students should be free to discover their own values. But he argued that if people freely conducted their own values searches, they would discover universal and timeless truths, such as sincerity, independence, and self-knowledge. These values, Rogers said, "appear to be common across individuals and perhaps even over cultures."[29]

Despite all this experimentation, there is little evidence that the high schools of the 1970s ended up making students either question authority or challenge moral precepts. A poll conducted by Daniel Yankelovich in 1973, for example, showed that while college students of the 1960s were willing to challenge the

34

old order, the principles of high school students were largely untouched by the turmoil of the decade.

Yankelovich asked high school students and college students their views on various ethical questions. When these students differed in their views, high school students tended to favor the moral position by about ten percentage points over their college-aged peers. For example, 68 percent of high school students surveyed said that America needed more law and order, and 67 percent thought there should be more respect for authority, but only 51 percent of college students favored more law and order, while only 48 percent thought that respect for authority needed to be increased. When compared with their college counterparts, 19 percent more high school students agreed that "hard work always pays off," and 12 percent more high school students endorsed "duty before pleasure" than did college students. And while both high schoolers and collegians Yankelovich surveyed thought that the three most important values were love, self-fulfillment, and friendship, high school students believed in work 14 percent more than college students, religion 22 percent more often, "a clean, moral life" 28 percent more often, and patriotism 34 percent more often than college students of the time did.[30]

If the 1970s was the decade of failed educational experiments, the 1980s was one of repeated attempts to return to the traditions the previous generation had thought were exhausted. In 1978, the state of Maryland convened a commission to determine what sorts of values should be taught in the schools; several other states, most notably California and Kentucky, have since followed suit. Some educators, in particular Edward Wynne of the University of Illinois (Chicago Circle), have called for high schools to implement moral codes defining what the school should stand for.

State school systems, had, of course, been requiring teachers to teach values of some sort for a very long time. A 1933 survey of the American Historical Association by Howard K. Beale found that states required that teachers teach benevolence, business integrity, chastity, cleanliness, common honesty, courtesy, economy, frugality, gentility, good behavior, honesty, humor, industry, integrity, justice, kindness, love of country, manners, moderation, moral courage, morality, and morals—and that was just the first half of the alphabet. In Nevada, for example, Beale found that the state required each teacher to teach "the preservation of songbirds, fish and game, and to teach and explain to such children of suitable ages, at least twice each school year, the fish and game laws of the state of Nevada."[31]

These codes were forgotten in the tumult of the 1960s. When they were reinvented in the 1970s and 1980s, the new codes differed in content, form, and nature. Maryland's Values Education Commission, for example, lists "respect for one's property" as a value; former Secretary of Education William Bennett includes "kindness, diligence, honesty, fairness, and respect for law."[32]

Edward Wynne and Mark Holmes have produced the most elaborate code. It calls for students to "develop their latent capacities to improve morally, intellectually, and socially" and "develop a confident awareness of self, including a judicious blend of self-respect, humility, and a sense of control of their own destiny."[33]

But what happens when elements of these codes conflict with each other? If "respect for law" is a universal moral value, does it follow that civil disobedience is unacceptable under any circumstances? Can one be kind and unfair? For although the values listed in moral codes "do not always oppose each other," notes Department of Education analyst Ivor Pritchard, "they do conflict often enough to produce serious dilemmas."[34]

A second barrier, legal and philosophical, comes from legal prohibitions against teaching religion in the schools. Teaching values without being able to refer to the Jewish and Christian roots from which they derive produces what Rockford Institute president Allan Carlson calls "cut-flower values"; attractive at first, they quickly wither and die. When "values are stripped away from their cultural contexts," Carlson told the *Washington Post*, "they don't have any life. They tend to become banal and not compelling to children."[35]

The 1980s also marked a resurgence of character education. Two small think tanks, the American Institute of Character Education of San Antonio, Texas, and the Thomas Jefferson Research Center of Pasadena, California, led this effort. The American Institute of Character Education claims that its curriculum is used in 40,000 classrooms across America; the Thomas Jefferson Research Center says that 34,000 classrooms use its publications. Such civic organizations as the Kiwanis Clubs donate the materials to the schools. The revival of character education differed substantially in form from its ancestors. The programs, for example, are shorter; a Thomas Jefferson Research Center brochure promises that it only takes ten minutes a day to build character.

But there are striking resemblances in content between the morality codes of the 1980s and those of the 1920s. A prize-winning morality code of 1926 (endorsed by the president of Yale and a Supreme Court justice) argued that "good Americans play fair, are self-reliant, do their duty," and "work in friendly cooperation with fellow workers." The "Twelve Steps to Success" issued by the Thomas Jefferson Research Center in 1990 calls for students to "be responsible, be confident, be a doer, be a tough worker."[36]

But even the character educators admit to disappointing results. In an interview, Thomas Jefferson Research Center executive vice president Patrick McCarthy said there was no evidence that students' characters were actually changed by his organization's publications, although there was some evidence that students who took character education classes tended to cut fewer classes and commit less vandalism; girls tended to become pregnant less often.

Character education today breaks with the past in one crucial respect—its emphasis on self-esteem. Self-esteem is a cornerstone of the character education movement of the 1990s. In the Thomas Jefferson Research Center's publication, *The Self-Esteem Repair and Maintenance Manual,* David Brooks and Rex Dalby urge students toward self-improvement through such exercises as listing all the traits they like and dislike about themselves and listing their goals in life. "The fact that you are here on this earth means that you are important and of value," say the authors. "You can feel good about yourself, you can reward yourself, and you can consciously improve yourself."[37]

The authors also offer uplifting quotations from Plato, John Greenleaf Whittier, Henry Ford, Ted Turner, and Susan Jeffers, Ph.D. ("Feel the fear and do it anyway").

In stressing self-esteem, the character educators are responding to market demand. In 1984, California appointed a commission designed to improve the self-esteem of citizens in that state; similar commissions have been appointed in Michigan, Maryland, Missouri, and Florida. The National Education Association has also endorsed "esteem-training" for students.

But, as Vanderbilt University education professor Chester Finn observes, students are feeling better about themselves and doing worse in school. In 1988, 80 percent of the high school seniors surveyed by the Institute of Social Research at the University of Michigan said they had a "positive attitude" towards life, and 79 percent said they were satisfied about themselves, but the National Assessment of Educational Progress reports that only 26 percent of the high school class of 1988 could write a persuasive letter, while one-third of these students did not know that the Mississippi River flows into the Gulf of Mexico. Given the "dismal achievement" and general happiness of most high school students, Finn asks, why would anyone conclude that "the nation's education problem lies in a deficit of self-esteem?"[38]

Perhaps the self-esteem movement exists as a quick fix to a deeply rooted problem. Four major studies conducted in the 1980s show the nature and extent of the decline in values among high school students. In the early 1980s, Joseph Adelson, a psychologist at the University of Michigan, led a team of researchers who interviewed 450 students in five nations to determine what they understood about politics. He concluded that although most adolescents could recite facts learned in class (such as the branches of government or the articles in the Bill of Rights), few understood those facts. "The young adolescent [may] have in his head many random bits of political information," Adelson contends, "without a secure understanding of those concepts that would give order and meaning to the information."[39]

The notion of an adolescent rebel plotting and scheming against authority, Adelson argues, is a romantic fiction, as most

38

adolescents tend to respect authority. What the teenagers Adelson interviewed did believe in were three principles: law and order, quality, and abundance—the notion that everything should be free, or that everyone should get credit cards with no spending limits. "Grievances against the system, when present, do not seem deeply held," Adelson observes. "The apocalyptic or chiliastic mentality so often imputed to adolescents is scarcely to be found."[40]

If Adelson is right, much of what character education does is unnecessary, since most students already respect the authority of teachers and principals. But if civics cannot be taught, Adelson's study leads to the conclusion first posed by Aristotle—that virtue cannot be taught. If most teenagers do not understand why democracy is the best form of government, can they be expected to comprehend right and wrong?

At the same time as Adelson conducted his study, the Institute for Social Research at the University of Michigan decided to determine the reasons why the children of Vietnamese immigrants, having survived the Vietnam War and Communist tyranny, did well in American schools. A team of psychologists led by Nathan Caplan visited Orange County, California, Seattle, Houston, Chicago, and Boston, interviewed parents, students, and teachers, and reviewed school transcripts.

Caplan and his colleagues found that large families helped Vietnamese students succeed. In most studies, Caplan reported, researchers found that each additional child in a family meant that that child had, on average, a 15 percent lower grade point average than the child's older brothers and sisters. But Caplan found that in Vietnamese families, the larger the family, the better children did in school. This was because parents insisted that children do their homework; "among the refugee families, homework clearly dominates household activities during weeknights."[41] Older brothers and sisters in Vietnamese families routinely helped their younger siblings with their studies; these older students "seem to learn as much from teaching as from being taught."[42] (Such behavior is highly unusual among American families; the National Assessment of Educational Progress reports that in 1990, 66 percent of twelfth graders surveyed reported that no one helped with their homework, and an additional 8 percent said that they did no homework at all.) On average, Vietnamese high school students spent three hours and ten minutes a night on homework, twice as much as the typical American high school student.

Caplan and his colleagues concluded that the success of Vietnamese students in the classroom shows that high schools still have the ability to educate. Where schools fail, in the opinion of Caplan and his colleagues, is in trying to teach values that should be taught by parents. "We believe that the view of our schools as failing to educate stems from the unrealistic demand that the educational system deal with urgent social service needs," Caplan wrote in an article in *Scientific American*. The increasing amount of time spent in telling students not to use drugs, not to get pregnant, not to be violent, and other nonacademic tasks "have consumed the scarce resources allocated to students and have compromised the schools' academic function. The primary role of teachers has become that of parent by proxy; they are expected to transform the attitude and behavior of children, many of whom come to school ill-prepared to learn."[43]

In a third study, commissioned for the Girl Scouts of America and conducted by a Louis Harris research team led by Harvard psychiatrist Robert Coles and University of Virginia sociologist James Davison Hunter, 5000 high school students were polled in the fall of 1989 on their moral beliefs. After examining the polling data, Coles and Hunter discovered that high school students have five sets of "moral compasses." These compasses tended, most of the time, to point students on the right path. Twenty-five percent of the students surveyed were Kohlbergian "civic humanists" who said their actions primarily resulted from a desire to advance the common good. Adelsonian "conventionalists" comprised 20 percent of the survey sample; these students followed the advice given by such authorities as parents and teachers. Sixteen percent of the sample were "theistic," saying that God and the Bible were their chief moral guides. Only 28 percent did not use a fixed moral standard, 18 percent saying they were "expressivists" whose chief concern was maximizing their happiness, and 10 percent were utilitarians who preferred to act in whatever manner would advance their careers. (The remaining 11 percent had no preference.)[44]

Students tended to be moral in the home and immoral in the classroom. While only 5 percent of high school students said they would steal from their parents, 65 percent said they would cheat on exams, and 38 percent said they would lie to protect a friend who had vandalized school property. (Only 24 percent said they would tell the truth about vandalism.) While 49 percent of the theists and 40 percent of the conventionalists would help an injured classmate, only 22 percent of the utilitarians and 32 percent of the expressivists would do the same. Girls tended to be more likely than boys to help others and to tell the truth.[45]

"When religion was removed from the schools, nothing came along to take its place," Coles writes. "Teachers were stripped of the moral authority they once had—in effect we have removed right and wrong from schools."[46]

Syracuse University sociologist Gerald Grant decided to explore the changes of American high schools by examining one high school, which he calls "Hamilton High." After a five-year study, including one year as a teacher at the school, Grant concluded that the legalisms resulting from "students' rights" decisions of the early 1970s resulted in the fundamental rule of Hamilton High concerning conduct: Everything not forbidden is permitted. The student handbook, for example, told students which acts were illegal (gambling, stealing) but said little about what they should strive for. The school "did not ask students to improve what they found, to extend a hand to others, to aspire to any ideals or worthy traditions." School assemblies did little to promote a sense of community. When a popular student died, the school did not hold an assembly but suggested that individual students turn to guidance counselors for private therapy sessions.[47]

Hamilton High was a "shopping mall" high school. Students who wanted to work hard and get a good education could do so; students who wished to be lazy and do little work were also free to follow that path, as long as they didn't break any laws and attended class regularly. But students were unsatisfied; they wished for adults to wield their authority and tell them what was right and wrong. One-third of the drug-using students surveyed in the early 1980s, for example, "expressed a latent yearning for more guidance by adults."[48] Other students wanted parents to spend more time urging students not to drive when drunk.

In my opinion, both Adelson and Coles are right. Students may well respect authority, but when parents, teachers, and principals abdicate their responsibilities, those students may allow their passions to lead them astray. One solution for schools interested in restoring morality might be to determine the moral codes that govern their communities, and then act to enforce them. But in creating these codes, principals, teachers, and administrators should not overreach themselves, trying to improve upon the Ten Commandments, but simply work to make their schools decent and humane places where students can be effective and productive.

A second solution might well be to return to teaching great works of literature. The school system that brought the *McGuffey's Readers* back to the classroom was on the right track; perhaps McGuffey is dated, but Nathaniel Hawthorne, William Shakespeare, and George Eliot have much to teach even the most jaded high school student. As Flannery O'Connor once noted, "A story is a way to say something that can't be said any other way—you tell a story because a statement would be inadequate."[49] Certainly more students have been improved by great literature than by catch phrases.

Creating a moral and effective school is a tricky, complex business. But a school where good books are regularly taught by honorable men and women would do a great deal to help students become decent and just.

NOTES

1. Wendell Berry, *What Are People For?* (San Francisco: North Point Press, 1990), p. 26.
2. Cited in Stephen Yulish, *The Search for a Civic Religion* (Washington, D.C.: University Press of America, 1980), p. 51.
3. Cited in Charles Glenn, *The Myth of the Common School* (Amherst: University of Massachusetts Press, 1988), p. 35.
4. Laura Sessions Stepp, "Morals Classes Urged in Schools," *Washington Post,* June 19, 1990.
5. Sonia L. Nazario, "Schoolteachers Say It's Wrongheaded to Try to Teach Students What's Right," *Wall Street Journal,* April 6, 1990.
6. Amy Gutmann, "Educating for [Multiple] Choice," *New Perspectives Quarterly,* Fall 1990, p. 49.
7. Tony P. Hall, "Teaching Values," *Congressional Record,* January 31, 1989.
8. Aristotle, *Nicomachean Ethics,* trans. W. D. Ross and J. O. Urmson. In *The Complete Works of Aristotle,* ed. Jonathan Barnes (Princeton: Princeton University Press, 1984), p. 1730 (1095a).
9. Cited in Ruth Miller Elson, *Guardians of Tradition: American Schoolbooks of the Nineteenth Century* (Lincoln, NB: University of Nebraska Press, 1964), p. 186.
10 Cited in David B. Tyack & Elisabeth Hansot, *Managers of Virtue* (New York: Basic Books, 1982), p. 75.
11. Cited in Gerald Grant, "Bringing the 'Moral' Back In," *NEA Today,* January 1989, p. 55.
12. Yulish, op.cit., pp. 112–113.
13. Character Education Inquiry, *Studies in the Organization of Character* (New York: Macmillan, 1929), vol. 2, p. 453.
14. Carl R. Rogers, "A Plan for Self-Directed Change in an Educational System,: *Educational Leadership,* May 1967.
15. Ibid.
16. Ibid.
17. Cited in Carl R. Rogers, *Freedom to Learn for the '80s* (Columbus, OH: Merrill, 1983), p. 235.
18. William R. Coulson, *A Sense of Community* (Columbus, OH: Merrill, 1973), p. 75. See also William K. Kilpatrick, *Why*

Johnny Can't Tell Right from Wrong (New York: Simon & Schuster, 1992), pp. 34–35.

19. Louis Raths, Merrill Hansen, & Sidney Simon, *Values and Teaching: Working with Values in the Classroom* (Columbus, OH: Merrill, 1978), pp. 33–34.
20. Ibid., p. 81.
21. Ibid., pp. 112–113.
22. Ibid., p. 185.
23. Cited in Martin Eger, "The Conflict in Moral Education: An Informal Case Study," *Public Interest*, Spring 1981. The author of the manual was Howard Kirschenbaum.
24. Alan L. Lockwood, "The Effects of Values Clarification and Moral Development Curricula on School-Age Subjects: A Critical Review of Recent Research," *Review of Educational Research*, Summer 1978.
25. Ivor Pritchard, *Moral Education and Character* (Washington, D.C.: Department of Education, 1988), p. 13.
26. From a Kohlberg essay in Ralph Mosher, ed. *Moral Education* (New York: Praeger, 1980), p. 56.
27. F. Clark Power, Ann Higgins, & Lawrence Kohlberg, *Lawrence Kohlberg's Approach to Moral Education* (New York: Columbia University Press, 1987), pp. 298–299.
28. Carl R. Rogers, "Beyond the Watershed: And Where Now?", *Educational Leadership*, May 1977.
29. Rogers, *Freedom to Learn for the '80s*, pp. 267–268.
30. Daniel Yankelovich, *The New Morality: A Profile of American Youth in the 70's* (New York : McGraw-Hill, 1974), pp. 90, 160.
31. Howard K. Beale, *Are American Teachers Free? An Analysis of Restraints Upon The Freedom of Teaching* (New York: Scribners, 1936), p. 323.
32. Ivor Pritchard, *Character Education: Research Prospects and Problems* (Washington, D.C.: U.S. Department of Education, 1988), p. 3.
33. Mark Holmes & Edward Wynne, *Making the Schools an Effective Community* (New York: Falmer Press, 1989), p. 75.
34. Pritchard, *Character Education*, p. 4.
35. Cited in E. J. Dionne, "Struggling to Find a Way to Teach Values," *Washington Post*, July 9, 1990.
36. From a Thomas Jefferson Research Center brochure, n.d.
37. B. David Brooks & Rex K. Dalby, *The Self-Esteem Repair and Maintenance Manual* (Newport Beach, CA: Kincaid House, 1990), pp. 3–4.

38. Chester E. Finn, Jr., "Narcissus Goes to School," *Commentary*, June 1990, p. 43.
39. Joseph Adelson, *Inventing Adolescence* (New Brunswick, NJ: Transaction, 1986), p. 217.
40. Ibid., p. 226.
41. Nathan Caplan, Marcella H. Choy, & John K. Whitmore, "Indochinese Refugee Families and Academic Achievement," *Scientific American*, February 1992, p. 39.
42. Ibid., pp. 39–40.
43. Ibid., p. 41.
44. *Girl Scouts Survey on the Beliefs and Moral Values of America's Children: Executive Summary* (New York: Girl Scouts of America, 1990), pp. 4–5.
45. Ibid., pp. 7–9.
46. Cited in *The Center Letter*, Thomas Jefferson Research Center, June-July 1990, p. 3.
47. Gerald Grant, *The World We Created at Hamilton High* (Cambridge, MA: Harvard University Press, 1988), pp. 107–108.
48. Ibid., p. 94.
49. Cited in William Kirk Kilpatrick, "The Use of Literature in Character Formation," in *Content, Character, and Choice in Schooling: Public Policy and Research Implications* (Washington, D.C.: National Council on Educational Research, 1986), p. 88.

3

THE
PROBLEMS
PRINCIPALS
FACE

"Of course, I follow them; I'm their leader."
Anonymous

One point in the continuing debate over education reform is the notion that, in effective schools, the principal functions not as a middle manager but as a leader whose actions mold and determine the school's conduct and culture. Such popular films as *The Principal* and *Stand by Me* depict principals as the modern equivalents of sheriffs in western movies, men capable of bringing order to an anarchic situation by use of their fists and their brains.

It may well be that the only principals capable of transforming schools, restoring order, or expelling delinquents are those created by Hollywood screenwriters. Over the past thirty years, principals have steadily lost power, authority, and clout. Central offices have bound them by regulations and red tape. Teachers' unions have enabled teachers to bypass principals' authority and undermine their power. Federal and state funding created positions and support staff principals cannot control. Court decisions forced them to conform to legalistic procedures in many of their actions. And many of the attempts to transform schools in the

47

1980s, particularly those implemented in the "first wave" of school reform from 1983 to 1985, ignored the problems principals face.

The result is that principals are the forgotten people of American education; most of the debate about high schools simply takes principals for granted. Yet principals are the key to ensuring a successful school. If principals are barred from exercising their independent initiative, how can schools be successfully reformed?

Principals were never fully independent actors, and calls to restrict the authority of central offices are not new. They are one of the recurring themes in the history of American education. As early as 1913, Ellwood P. Cubberley, a professor of education at Stanford, saw that principals were being hampered by regulations. Hired to study the schools in Portland, Oregon, Cubberley observed that principals were guided by eight pages of rules, including the requirement that they be at their schools precisely one hour early in case of cold weather. "Both in letter and in spirit the functions imposed on principals are routine and clerical," Cubberley wrote. "The system...fails utterly to encourage, much less does it require, the assumption of real educational responsibility, the exercise of professional initiative and originality by principals."[1] For the rest of his life Cubberley strived to ensure that principals achieved as much independence as possible. "Whatever can be done to add strength and dignity and responsibility to the office should be done, with the view to making each principal feel that his work is large and important," Cubberley wrote in 1929. "The knowledge, insight, skill and qualities for helpful leadership of the principal of the school practically determine the ideals and standards of achievements of both teachers and pupils within the school."[2]

Cubberley's prescient advice went unheeded because, at the time, it was largely unnecessary. In most cases, principals felt free to give orders and make decisions without being overruled by the board of education or the courts. They also strived as part of their jobs to be part of their communities. For example, when University of Chicago sociologist August Hollingshead spent 1941 and 1942 studying the citizens of a rural Illinois city he

48

called Elmtown, he observed that the principal of the high school had strong ties to the community through his membership in the Rotary Club and the town's Methodist church, where he sang in the choir "for policy's sake." The principal, moreover, not only personally advised parents when children cut class, but also physically punished students who missed detention. While members of the local gangs talked about beating up the principal in retaliation, Hollingshead remarked, they limited their comments to drawing "derogatory pictures."[3]

Most principals in the 1930s and 1940s felt comfortable in their positions. A typical memoir of the time was that of Frank P. Whitney, principal at Collinwood High School in Cleveland between 1935 and 1955. The principal, Whitney wrote, was freed "by an efficient central administration from most of the difficult problems of finance and public relations and ... by capable teachers from the laborious routine of classroom instruction." His "middle position [is] the most advantageous of all for the promotion of the great ends of education and life itself."[4]

Principals had reason to be happy; the school, after all, was their domain. Once a principal made a decision, parents, teachers, and students had little recourse. Until the 1960s, observe scholars Frederick Wirt and Michael Kirst, "an administrator's response to any student even politely questioning why he or she had to dress, walk, eat, speak, and otherwise act in the prescribed manner was much like that of writer Ring Lardner when his children questioned him: 'Shut up, I explained.'"[5]

But beginning in 1960, the principal's "middle position" began to erode. The first assault on the principal's power came from the rising militancy of teachers' unions. Unions did not take over the schools, but the authority unions gained was largely taken from the principals. Moreover, union-supported restrictions on teacher firing further hampered principals' ability to lead.

In 1960 the National Education Association (NEA) considered itself a professional organization that supplied services and held conferences. Its smaller rival, the American Federation of Teachers (AFT), was a loosely bound confederacy of big-city union locals that had not yet cohered into a national force. But in

1960, previously unaffiliated teachers in New York City were organized into the United Federation of Teachers, which became the AFT's largest local. In December 1960, and again in April 1962, these teachers did something rarely done until then—they went out on strike. These strikes proved to be quite popular. In 1965, there were nine strikes involving 1,720 teachers; by 1975, 218 strikes involved 182,300 teachers. At first, most of these strikes were conducted by the AFT. Seeing the gains made by their rivals, NEA affiliates switched their allegiance and became AFT locals in several of America's large cities, most notably New York and Philadelphia. In response, the NEA leadership first began to advocate collective bargaining (a decision not made until 1962), but soon became as committed to unionization as its rival.

Many of these strikes involved issues that today would not be disputed. The 1962 New York teachers' strike was over the role teachers should play in making decisions in their schools (a precursor of what is now known as "school-based management"). New York's teachers, for example, struck in 1967 over the issue of whether teachers could expel unruly students. In a less divisive age than the 1960s, teacher militancy might well not have occurred. But as United Federation of Teachers leader John O'Neill noted in 1966, "Public agencies move only in crisis, so we had to create one."[6] The end result of NEA and AFT agitation was that the union contract became an integral part of the corporate culture of high schools.

The best research on how the rise of teachers' unions affected high schools was conducted by Susan Moore Johnson in the late 1970s. Surveying dozens of high schools, she discovered few cases where a union had forced radical change on a school. In general, the process of unionization was gradual, and grievances were reasonable.

But principals lost ground steadily, at least in most cases. Few teachers, for example, felt willing to do overtime duty if it was not authorized by the union contract. Further, a rising number of union officials were placed in central offices to administer contracts. In New York City, Mayor John Lindsay put union members on city payrolls, claiming that the time union members spent administering contracts was "time devoted to the public interest." As a result, the city pays the salaries of six members of the United Federation of Teachers and provides pensions for twenty-seven others, even though the union collects a hefty $46 from each teacher each month in mandatory dues.[7] While the union members do not, as a rule, directly control principals, the regulations they produce to enforce a contract further limit the power of the principals.

Faced with a world where challenges to a contract resulted in extensive hearings and red tape, many of the principals surveyed by Johnson gave up much of their independent initiative. Other principals felt even more frustrated when it took grievance procedures to force bureaucracies to perform when principals on their own could do nothing. In one high school Johnson examined, a leaky roof remained unrepaired for years, despite numerous requests. The principal admitted to Johnson that if the union were to file a grievance procedure, the roof would be fixed. "Now isn't that sad?" the principal said. "When my teachers come to me and say, 'We know you've tried. Now let us try,' then I know they have more authority than I."[8]

Despite these encroachments on the authority of principals, the teachers Johnson interviewed did not want their principals to be wimps. Teachers, Johnson noted, "were critical of laissez-faire principals who relinquished too much power. . . . Teachers did not want to run the schools, but they were prepared to support a principal who demonstrated that their schools could be run well."[9]

If teachers were becoming more demanding, students were becoming more strident. This stridency resulted in a series of major decisions in which the Supreme Court declared that students had rights that should be respected. While these court decisions did not, in themselves, impede the principals' authority to act, they drew the line that principals could not cross. If, after 1970, principals had to discipline students "by the book," it was a book whose text was based on court rulings.

In *Tinker v. Des Moines* (1969), the Supreme Court ruled that suspending four high school students who wore black armbands to protest the Vietnam war was unconstitutional because the action violated the students' right to free speech. But the decision was not as clearcut as it first appeared. Although the Court declared that in certain situations suspensions could be used to block student actions, as when they created "substantial interference with schoolwork or discipline," it failed to define what "substantial" meant, thus resulting in considerable litigation. In 1975, the Supreme Court, in *Goss v. Lopez*, went farther in expanding students' rights. In *Lopez*, the Court overturned a principal's decision to suspend nine seniors for spiking the punch during a school prom by declaring that a student given a suspension of more than fourteen days must have a formal hearing to validate the suspension. Not to do so, the Court ruled, violated a student's right of due process. At the same time, the Court worried that this ruling—the *Lopez* decision—might result in endless litigation. "The prospect of imposing elaborate hearing requirements in every suspension case is viewed with great concern," noted Justice Byron White in stating the decision of the majority.[10]

But insofar as the impact on schools was concerned, in the wake of *Tinker* and *Lopez*, circuit and district courts were making decisions that, in years past, would have been made by principals and school boards. According to historian David Tyack, the number of court cases involving students (including disputes about discipline, curriculum, truancy, and compulsory attendance laws) increased from 554 in the 1957 to 1966 period to 1,691 between 1967 and 1976.[11] In most cases, courts acted to uphold authority: circuit courts ruled that suspending a student for yelling "He's a prick" at a vice principal at a shopping mall was valid (*Fenton v. Stear*, 1976); that reducing the grades of students caught drinking on a field trip was acceptable (*New Braunfels v. Armhe*, 1983); and that a student carrying a switchblade to the classroom could be indefinitely suspended (*McClain v. Lafayette County Board of Education*, 1982). In the most peculiar case following *Lopez*, a circuit court in 1983 (*Bernstein v. Menard*) ruled that a mother could not sue a high school for expelling her child from the school band.

And in most cases since *Lopez*, the Supreme Court has declared that schools generally have the constitutional authority to discipline troubled students. The Court has found that administrators cannot be routinely sued for violating students' constitutional rights when a student was suspended (*Wood v. Strickland*, 1975); that corporal punishment was not "cruel and unusual" (*Ingraham v. Wright*, 1977); that suspended students could not sue the schools for violating due-process laws unless the student was physically harmed (*Carey v. Pipkus*, 1978); and that a student's First Amendment rights were not violated after he was suspended for giving a speech at a high school assembly full of lewd, but not obscene, references (*Bethel School District v. Fraser*, 1986).

In the Court's strongest check on the *Lopez* decision, the Court, in *Board of Education v. McCluskey* (1982), ruled that a student's suspension for excessive alcohol consumption was constitutionally valid, even though the student was suspended under a rule that prohibited the use, sale, possession, or consumption of "narcotics or other hallucinogens, drugs, or controlled substances," but did not specifically forbid alcohol consumption. If a school board's discipline policy was reasonable, the Court ruled, a court could not substitute a judicially written discipline policy for any existing school discipline regulation.

But even while upholding the power of administrators, the courts ensured that the lawyer would still be a force in the high school. In *New Jersey v. T.L.O.* (1985), the Supreme Court considered the case of a 14-year-old girl who was caught smoking in a bathroom. Upon searching her purse, a vice principal discovered rolling papers, marijuana, a roll of dollar bills, and an index card headed "People Who Owe Me Money." The vice principal turned "T.L.O." over to the police, and she was subsequently convicted of drug dealing.

The New Jersey Supreme Court overturned the conviction, arguing that the search of T.L.O.'s purse was illegal because the vice principal did not have a warrant. The Supreme Court upheld T.L.O.'s conviction but said that students were protected by the Fourth Amendment ban on unreasonable searches and seizures. Only when there was a "reasonable suspicion" that a student was engaging in illicit activity, the Court declared, could a search be conducted. But by not defining this "reasonable suspicion" standard, the Court once again opened the door for litigation.[12]

And in *Honig v. Doe* (1988) the Court, by a 6 to 2 margin, ruled that "emotionally disturbed students" (defined under rules created as part of the Education for All Handicapped Children Act) could not be suspended for more than ten days, even though one student was caught fighting and another sexually harassed dozens of women students.

The result of these court cases was twofold. First, a successful principal must be a master of the law. As William Sparkman, a professor of education at Texas Tech, notes, principals not only need to understand constitutional law (particularly the ramifications of the First, Fourth, and Fourteenth amendments) but also the Civil Rights Act of 1964, tort legislation, the laws governing the rights of the handicapped, and the legal status of nontraditional families. Second, the end result of most of these laws was, in cases without precedent, to penalize action. Why take steps to punish a student or get rid of a bad teacher if the result was an endless and costly legal battle?

By 1980, principalship was at its lowest ebb. Using a method known as "open-systems analysis," the graduate schools of education taught that principals were the victims of ambiguous, chaotic, uncertain, and unpredictable social forces beyond their power to influence or control. And in the most extensive analysis ever conducted of how principals function, a team of researchers at the University of Illinois (Chicago) led by Van Cleve Morris spent 1980 and 1981 examining principals in that state and discovered that in most cases principals were shirking time-honored duties. Few principals that Morris and his associates studied, for example, bothered to spend time observing how teachers taught. "Evaluating teaching is generally a very unpleasant task," they observed. "Standing in judgment of other people is always difficult, especially when the judge (the teacher) has attended a teacher training institution and knows as much about pedagogy as any principal."[13]

As for parents, they were at best tolerated, at worst ignored. While the principals thought parents might occasionally be useful as volunteers, far too often they had to deal with a mother "whose self-appointed role goes beyond augmenting the staff." This sort of woman is "not interested in schedules, union contracts, central office bulletins or other constraints of organizational life. Her suggestions, therefore, seem crazy, because they contradict what is possible organizationally."[14]

To survive the petty demands of the central office, the best principals practiced what Morris and his associates called "creative insubordination." In one high school in the Chicago suburbs, the principal was given a federally required form to determine the racial composition of the school's student body. Taking the requirements of the form literally, the principal distributed it to his students. When the form was returned, one-sixth of the students surveyed declared that they were Aleuts or Eskimos. But such creativity was rare. Far too often, Morris and his associates reported, principals, faced with the "seeming bureaucratic aimlessness" of many initiatives, adopted "a low profile, paper-shuffling, keep-the-lid-on-and-the-boss-happy style of caretaker management."[15]

Clearly, paper shufflers and caretakers were hardly the best people to lead high schools. Several major studies published in the late 1970s and 1980s concluded that successful schools were precisely those where the principal took charge.

In 1979, a team of British researchers led by psychologist Michael Rutter published *Fifteen Thousand Hours*, detailing the results of a four-year examination of British high schools. They discovered that students had higher test scores in schools where decisions were made "at a senior level rather than in the staffroom." Rutter and his colleagues also discovered that "exam successes were more frequent and delinquency less common" when discipline policies were set by the school rather than left to individual teacher initiative.[16]

In *High School Achievement* (1982) and *Public and Private High Schools* (1987), James S. Coleman, a sociologist at the University of Chicago, and Thomas Hoffer, a researcher at Northern Illinois University, contended that private high schools (particularly Catholic ones) outperformed their public high school counterparts largely because private high schools were "functional communities" where parents have shared values and motives for placing their children in school. In contrast, Coleman and Hoffer argued, students in public high schools have nothing in common

55

except that they live in a particular area. Thus public high schools lacked "social capital," and their students did less well than their private high school counterparts. To build communities, said Coleman and Hoffer, principals should create opportunities for students, parents, and teachers to work together. Teachers and principals should meet frequently with parents and other community leaders, they advised, and principals should hold assemblies celebrating student achievements.[17]

In *Politics, Markets, and America's Schools* (1990), Brookings Institution senior fellow John Chubb and Stanford political scientist Terry Moe determined that where principals had a substantial degree of autonomy and vision, schools were effective; whereas where central offices or superintendents restrained principals from independent initiative, schools tended to be less effective. In 92.1 percent of the ineffective schools, central offices had above-average control over the firing and transfer of teachers; in effective schools, central offices handled firing only 43.6 percent of the time. In ineffective schools, unions dominated the process of hiring 52.3 percent of the time; in effective schools, unions were in control of hiring 13 percent of the time.[18] But even though autonomous principals perform better than those bound by regulations and the central office, Chubb and Moe reported that the trends in school administration were against giving principals more autonomy. Most of the changes proposed in the "first wave" of school reform in 1983/84—tougher graduation requirements, longer school days, greater emphasis on homework, a more difficult process of teacher certification, and so forth—did little to help the principal, since they in no way altered the process of teacher hiring and firing. These recommendations, passed down from national commissions, to state boards of education, to the district offices, did little to help principals who were given no say in the changes. After 1984, principals were faced with teachers with seemingly better qualifications, but they were still would-be generals who had no control over the troops. The result, said Chubb and Moe, was that most public high schools could not be true communities because their staffs were assembled by bureaucratic fiat. "For the most part, the principal is stuck with the teachers the system gives him. They are stuck with him. And the teachers are stuck with one another."[19]

The findings of Chubb and Moe are partially supported by the decennial survey conducted by the National Association of Secondary School Principals, a professional association located in Reston, Virginia. In the two volumes of *High School Leaders* (1988, 1990) a team of researchers led by Leonard Pellicer of the University of South Carolina surveyed principals across America and determined that much of the alarm about principals was justified.

By 1987, when the survey was conducted, many of the fads and trends of the 1960s had faded. The schools were no longer overrun by outside groups with their own agendas. The three most common groups principals said influenced them in a "moderate" or "extreme" way were athletic boosters (61 percent), band supporters (61 percent), and teachers' organizations (60 percent). Among the groups with the least influence were women's or minority rights organizations (12 percent), local labor organizations (10 percent), legal aid groups (7 percent), and censorship groups (books, programs, and so forth) (4 percent).[20]

But the burdens on principals—many of them due to regulation and paperwork—were still heavy. Eighty-three percent of the principals surveyed said they spent too much time on administrative details, and 69 percent considered new state guidelines and requirements burdensome—only slightly less than the 70 percent who complained about "apathetic and irresponsible parents."[21]

Principals' authority was also steadily being reduced. Thirty-three percent said they had little or no authority to hire teachers, 42 percent had little control over staffing practices, and 39 percent had no say over the budget. In contrast, in 1977, only 8 percent of the principals were limited in hiring teachers, 32 percent couldn't tell the teachers how to teach, and 33 percent were blocked from budget discussions.[22]

Yet despite these burdens, principals were largely happy. Surprisingly, job satisfaction has increased over time. Sixty-six percent of principals surveyed reported "considerable" satisfaction with their jobs, up from 48 percent in 1965; and 69 percent

57

say their job has a considerable amount of prestige, up from 50 percent in 1965. While the reason for this leap in satisfaction is not certain (perhaps the job has strong appeal for people who enjoy positions that lack responsibility), it is not due to money; adjusted for inflation, principals are earning the same pay they were getting ten years ago.

But can these happy principals be called leaders? Can they inspire students as did their predecessors in earlier generations? These questions are more complex than might appear at first glance. High schools are not the same organizations they were in the days of August Hollingshead or Frank Whitney. The modern high school is loaded with a multitude of programs and support staff—pregnancy prevention counselors, drug treatment staffers, handicapped instructors—whose funds and ultimate authority rest in the state capital or in Washington, D.C. Because of these programs and the large increase in electives, a principal has to oversee a far larger and more complex corporate culture than did his counterpart in 1960.

Researchers, however, have determined ways principals can become better leaders. Simply being visible and available to the staff helps a good deal. In a 1989 study from the Association for Supervision and Curriculum Development, Wilma T. Smith and Richard Andrews reported that being seen frequently by staff and students was "the most important factor" in ensuring that a principal be considered a "strong instructional leader." Principals that teachers considered strong, said Smith and Andrews, established a "visible presence" in schools 93 percent of the time; weak principals established their presence only 46 percent of the time.[23]

Other researchers are beginning to use time-tested techniques from management theory, popularized by Peter Drucker and Tom Peters, in the schools. In a 1990 study from the U.S. Department of Education, Terrence E. Deal of Peabody College, Vanderbilt University, and Kent D. Peterson of the University of Wisconsin (Madison) argued that treating a high school as a corporate culture and gradually making it more effective could, in the long run, be a better strategy than imposing policies from outside. "Bureaucratically implementing a reform policy can become a superficial exercise in compliance that never disturbs the underlying operations of schools," they contended.[24]

In Deal and Peterson's view, the symbolic aspects of the principalship have been critically neglected. Simple actions have long-term consequences, and the successful principal can act to ensure that even "seemingly innocuous actions" can be performed with a touch of *gravitas*. A daily tour of the building or a staff meeting can either be a chore or "a symbolic expression of the deeper values the principal holds for the school."[25] The walls and location of the principal's office, as well as his or her clothes, memo-writing style, demeanor ("a wink following a reprimand can have as much effect as the verbal reprimand itself"), and personal idiosyncrasies all determine whether a principal is revered or reviled.

The effective school is portrayed by Deal and Peterson as one where ceremonies matter. These ceremonies should reach out to the community, reaffirm the school's purpose, and serve as symbols to transmit values. An inspiring example is related by the authors. Frank Boyden, legendary founder of Deerfield Academy, in an annual assembly told the story of Tom Ashley, an exemplary student and teacher at the school who died in the brutal First World War battle of Chateau-Thierry. By recalling Ashley's life, Boyden transmitted the virtues that Ashley—and the school—stood for to future generations.

Deal and Peterson also find the case histories of other principals of interest. They find Hank Cotton, principal of Cherry Creek High School in the Denver suburbs and Bob Mastruzzi of Kennedy High School in New York City to be inspiring leaders. Cotton, in his first year after taking control of his troubled school, suspended 235 students for cutting classes, eliminated dozens of elective courses, and freed teachers from most of their nonteaching duties, such as monitoring the halls and cafeterias. (Cotton called such paper-generating duties "administrivia.") Mastruzzi revitalized the culture of his high school by giving prizes for high attendance, having students and teachers collect presents at Christmas for the poor and unfortunate, and by sponsoring the Special Olympics.

But bureaucratic and cultural obstacles ensure that such

principals are the exception rather than the rule. As Susan Moore Johnson observes, the history of most public high schools "is confined to the construction date chiselled above the door and a trophy case standing in the front hall."[26] She believes that most public high schools have lost their history irrevocably; the few time-honored observances schools retain are tied to religious holidays. If schools have lost their past and can only celebrate events with no Jewish or Christian roots (the "holiday concert" instead of the Christmas concert), what traditions can be established? "Large schools dependent on a public bureaucracy cannot be intimate settings where school leaders inspire others with visions of what a school might become," she contends.[27]

Moreover, while principals can certainly take many helpful actions on their own, a powerful central office can easily block these actions and demote or transfer principals. Principals fret at such rule from above; in a 1987 survey from the National Center for Education Information, the three organizations principals were most likely to name as groups who prevented them from "doing their jobs the way they would like" were teachers' unions, state departments of education, and the U.S. Department of Education.[28]

Principals' frustration about their bosses is understandable, because such centralized control pervades high schools with an aura of remoteness and inflexibility. The school concerns of superintendents and school boards are not those of parents. In 1991 the *American School Board Journal* surveyed school superintendents and school board members about what they want schools to do, and compared the results with the annual Gallup poll on education. As of January 1991, school board members were chiefly concerned with facilities (37 percent), satisfying state mandates (36 percent), and devising a curriculum (30 percent). Parents were primarily concerned with drug use (38 percent), lack of discipline (17 percent), and school finances (13 percent).[29]

But if and when power is devolved, principals may come under the control of teachers by bureaucratic fiat, and also be bound by regulations. In Chicago, for example, parent-teacher councils recently acquired the authority to hire and fire principals, ending the long-established practice of giving principals tenure for life. Two hundred principals were hired by these councils in Chicago between January 1990 and February 1991; 18 percent of the city's principals quit rather than face the councils.

If, moreover, these principals attempt to take any action, they must still wend their way through a bureaucratic maze. To change a bus stop location, for example, a principal must request permission from a district coordinator, who forwards the request to the Chicago Department of Education's transportation bureau, who may take up to sixty days to render a decision. Principals in Chicago also have no control over janitors, cafeteria workers, and school bus drivers, as these city employees are controlled by their separate union contracts.[30]

But if a principal can't pick teachers, restore lapsed traditions, or even tell the cafeteria to stop serving Swiss chard, that does not mean that principals are doomed to be ineffectual. Principals can change school cultures somewhat, but these changes are slow and incremental. Further, a principal interested in transforming a school must establish his will early and understand that the role of leader is one that cannot be assumed but must be earned.

Without changes in school bureaucracy, the changes principals can effect are minimal. As evidence, consider a report issued by the RAND Corporation in 1990 about New York City high schools. Like James Coleman and John Chubb before them, RAND researchers Paul T. Hill, Gail E. Foster, and Tamar Gendler discovered that Catholic high schools and public high schools with clear purposes and missions produce better achieving students than "zoned" high schools locked into bureaucratic hierarchies. In the average New York high school, RAND reports, students routinely roam the halls wearing Walkmans; tardiness is not only the rule but diligent students who want to get to class on time cannot, since a directive from the central office only allows three minutes between classes. Students not only do little work (failing two classes is considered standard) but in class students frequently eat, talk, rummage through purses, and even walk out. On pleasant spring days, average class attendance falls from twenty-five to five. While teachers

61

record attendance (as required by their contracts), little is done to reinforce discipline since, in most cases, the school has no record of the addresses and telephone numbers of the parents of frequent absentees. Classrooms are littered with candy wrappers and soda cans, and the halls are occasionally defaced with graffiti.

In zoned schools, teachers and students operate under the rule that "adults agree not to demand too much in return for the students' agreement not to cause trouble."[31] Principals in New York not only have no power to hire teachers, but cannot even be sure how many teachers he will have at any given time. As students drop out throughout the year, departments are cut (by up to 20 percent) and teachers reassigned. Efforts by principals to change the system "require tremendous amounts of paperwork, physical and emotional energy, and often fail anyway."[32]

How does a "zoned" school become one with a mission and purpose? The first step, say the RAND researchers, is for central offices to delegate "budgetary and staffing decisions to the school-site level."[33] The central office "must become less a regulatory and evaluative organization and more a facilitator of school-level problem solving."[34]

For left unchecked, central offices will grow endlessly. In Washington, D.C., the school board responded to financial pressures by hiring 1,050 administrators and threatening to fire up to 800 teachers. R. David Hall, president of the Washington, D.C., school board, explained to the *Washington Post* that it would be hard to reduce the central office because of civil service rules about seniority. "If we abolished positions with people in them, all of those people would bump other people, and if they bump an existing classroom teacher or principal, the loser is the child," Hall said.[35]

Such thinking must change if the authority principals once had is to be restored. The reforms needed to turn principals into leaders and high schools into places with clear and definable missions will not be produced in Washington, D.C., or the state capitals. They will be made in central offices across America. Only when devolution of power, either through school-based management or through choice, becomes permanent will principals be free to lead.

62

NOTES

1. *The Portland Survey: A Textbook on City School Administration Based on a Concrete Study* (Yonkers-on-Hudson, NY: World Book, 1915), p. 156.
2. Ellwood P. Cubberley. *Public School Administration: A Statement of the Fundamental Principles Underlying the Organization and Administration of Public Education*. Revised edition. (Boston, MA: Houghton Mifflin, 1929), p. 295.
3. August B. Hollingshead, *Elmtown's Youth and Elmtown Revisited* (New York, NY: Wiley, 1975), p. 139.
4. Frank P. Whitney, *School and I: The Autobiography of an Ohio Schoolmaster* (Yellow Springs, OH: Antioch Press, 1957), pp. 49–50.
5. Frederick W. Kirt & Michael P. Wirst, *Schools in Conflict: The Politics of Education* (Champaign, IL: University of Illinois Press, 1987), p. 29.
6. Quoted in Alan Rosenthal, *Pedagogues and Power: Teacher Groups in School Politics* (Syracuse, NY: Syracuse University Press, 1969), p. 77.
7. John Hellman, "How to Cut the Budget," *New York*, January 21, 1991, p. 29.
8. Susan Moore Johnson, *Teachers Unions in Schools* (Philadelphia: Temple University Press, 1984), p. 54.
9. Ibid., p. 163.
10. Cited in Kern Alexander & M. David Alexander, *American Public School Law* (St. Paul, MI: West, 1985), p. 319.
11. David Tyack, Thomas Jones, & Aaron Benavot, *Law and the Shaping of Public Education, 1785-1954* (Madison, WI: University of Wisconsin Press, 1987), pp. 217–218.
12. Alexander & Alexander, op. cit., p. 338. See also Perry A. Zirkel & Sharon Nalbone Richardson, *A Digest of Supreme Court Decisions Affecting Education*, second edition (Bloomington, IN: Phi Delta Kappa Educational Foundation, 1988).
13. Van Cleve Morris, Robert L. Crowson, Cynthia Porter-Gehrie, & Emanuel Hurwitz, Jr., *Principals in Action: The Reality of Managing Schools* (Columbus, OH: Merrill, 1984), p. 58.
14. Ibid., p. 122.
15. Ibid., p. 163.
16. Michael Rutter, Barbara Maughan, Peter Mortimore, Janet

Ouston, with Alan Smith, *Fifteen Thousand Hours: Secondary Schools and their Effect on Children* (Cambridge, MA: Harvard University Press, 1979), p. 192.

17. James S. Coleman & Thomas Hoffer, *Public and Private High Schools: The Effect of Communities* (New York: Basic Books, 1987), pp. 236–238.

18. John H. Chubb & Terry M. Moe, *Politics, Markets, and America's Schools* (Washington, D.C.: Brookings Institution, 1990), p. 154.

19. Ibid., p. 50.

20. Leonard O. Pellicer, Lorin W. Anderson, James W. Keefe, Edgar A. Kelly, & Lloyd E. McCleary, *High School Leaders and their Schools. Volume I: A National Profile* (Reston, VI: National Association of Secondary School Principals, 1988), p. 157.

21. Ibid., p. 155.

22. Ibid.

23. Wilma Smith & Richard Andrews, *Instructional Leadership: How Principals Make a Difference* (Alexandria, VA: Association for Supervision and Curriculum Development, 1989), p. 37.

24. Terence E. Deal & Kent D. Peterson, *The Principal's Role in Shaping School Culture* (Washington, D.C.: U.S. Department of Education, 1990), p. 6.

25. Ibid., p. 21.

26. Susan Moore Johnson, *Teachers at Work: Achieving Success in Our Schools* (New York: Basic Books, 1990), p. 281.

27. Ibid., p. 245.

28. C. Emily Feistritzer, *Profile of School Administrators in the U.S.* (Washington, D.C.: National Center for Education Information, 1988), p. 85.

29. "What Boards Value," *American School Board Journal,* January 1991, pp. 37–42.

30. Mark Lawrence Ragan, "People Power Blows Change into Chicago," *Insight,* March 25, 1991, p. 51.

31. Paul T. Hill, Gail E. Foster, & Tamar Gendler, *High Schools with Character* (Santa Monica, CA: RAND, 1990), p. 24.

32. Ibid.

33. Ibid., p. 73.

34. Ibid., p. 77.

35. Lynda Richardson, "Ordered Cut, D.C. School Staff Grew," *Washington Post,* April 20, 1991.

4

THE
PROBLEMS
TEACHERS
FACE

"The Schoolmasters [should] consider themselves as in
the place of Parents to the children under their care . . . that
they frequently address their pupils on moral and religious
subjects, endeavoring to impress their minds with a sense of
the being and providence of God, and the obligations they
have to love, serve, and pray to Him; [with] their duty to
their parents and masters; the beauty and excellence of truth,
justice, and mutual love."[1]

"Instructions to the Schoolmasters," adopted by Boston in 1789

"On the average we get about 2 percent efficiency out
of schoolbooks as they are written today. The education of
the future, as I see it, will be conducted through the medium
of the motion picture . . . where it should be possible to obtain
100 percent efficiency."[2]

Thomas A. Edison (1922)

"School is a conflict—mean and miserable—and I hate
conflicts. I was never born to command; I do not want to
command. . . . I can be cruel, but not stern. So I struggle with
my nature and with my class till I feel all frayed into rags.

Think of a quivering greyhound set to mind a herd of pigs and you see my teaching."[3]
D.H. Lawrence, frustrated middle school teacher

"If, then, the manners of the teacher are to be imitated by the pupils—if he is the glass, at which they 'do dress themselves,' how strong is the necessity, that he should understand those nameless and innumerable practices, in regard to deportment, dress, conversation, and all personal habits, that constitute the difference between a gentleman and a clown. We can bear some oddity, or eccentricity in a friend whom we admire for his talents, or revere for his virtues; but it becomes quite a different thing, when the oddity, or the eccentricity, is to be the pattern or model, from which fifty or a hundred children are to form their manners."
Fourth Annual Report of the Boston Board of Education (1841)[4]

Teachers have largely been forgotten in the debate over American education reform. Most of the issues discussed in American education do not address the performance of teachers. The quality of American teaching and the changing psychology of the classroom do not enter into discussions of school organization or structure.

But it is clear that, over the past half century, the American high school teacher's authority has steadily waned. Among the disadvantageous influences are students who have increasingly become bored, impudent, and less willing to learn; administrators who smother teachers in red tape and fail to back them in disciplinary actions; and regulations imposed by state and local boards of education ensure that teachers' jobs steadily become more demanding, more frustrating, and less interesting.

Faced with a loss of respect, autonomy, and dignity, teachers are fleeing the classroom or suffering burnout—hardly surprising, given the worsening work conditions most teachers have to endure. As Gerald Grant, a professor of education and sociology at Syracuse, observed, "plumbers or auto workers would shut down a job by noon if they faced the insult and abuse that many teachers routinely encounter."[5]

Teacher frustration with their jobs is not new. As the twentieth century has progressed, the abilities and eagerness of students to learn has steadily declined. The first known instance of "dumbing down" tests, for example, took place in Boston as far back as 1919. The city attempted to administer a test to eighth grade honor students previously given in 1845, but had to change 82 percent of the questions because the nineteenth-century test was too difficult for their school generation.

By the 1920s, standards in American high schools were in steady decline. When Robert S. Lynd and Helen Staughton Lynd studied the high school in the city they called Middletown, they discovered that academic classes were being replaced by "practical" ones; "commercial English" was far more popular than courses in English literature. While 20 percent of Middletown's high school students still took Latin, this was largely because the Latin classes produced a popular annual pageant. (The businessmen in Middletown thought Latin "deader than last summer's straw hat."[6]) By 1924, the Lynds observed, teachers were not the "wise, skilled, revered elders" they had been in the past. "In this commercial culture the 'teacher' and 'professor' do not occupy the position they did even a generation ago."[7]

Further, and perhaps more deadly, the education bureaucracy was beginning to develop. In 1890, the superintendent of Middletown's schools was the only administrator who did not teach. By 1925, there were several layers of administrators who never set foot in the classroom. "In personnel as well as in textbooks and courses of study," the Lynds wrote, "strains or maladjustments in education are being met by further elaboration and standardization."[8]

Standards continued to fall. By 1930, two-thirds of American high schools had abandoned medieval history, and one-third stopped teaching ancient history. By 1933, the U.S. Office of Education reported that more than half of U.S. high school teachers routinely promoted students they thought were failures. In the 1930s, historian David K. Cohen observed, "most students seem not to have wanted a heavy academic diet, and in general they got what they wanted."[9]

But even though standards were declining, most students received at least a basic education. As Frank Armbruster of the

Hudson Institute wrote, "even the 'dumbest' kids in the vast classes of second-and-third generation immigrant pupils from neighborhoods stuck in poverty could read, know the multiplication tables, and handle straightforward arithmetic problems."[10]

Most high school teachers fifty years ago were single women—in 1940 only 12 percent were men. And their communities expected them to maintain strict moral standards. Until World War I, theater-going was largely forbidden; in the 1920s many rural areas and small towns frowned on their teachers playing cards or dancing; eleven teachers were fired in Ottawa, Kansas, by officials in 1929 when they were caught at a local country club dance. Perhaps the most extreme case was a North Carolina town of the 1920s that required the women who taught in their schools to sign a contract that stated: "I promise not to go out with any young men except in so far as it may be necessary to stimulate Sunday-school work. I promise not to fall in love, to become secretly engaged or secretly married. . . . I promise to sleep at least eight hours a night, to eat carefully, and to take every precaution to keep in the best of health and spirits in order that I may be better able to render efficient service to my pupils."[11]

A survey conducted by Howard K. Beale for the American Historical Association in 1933 found that these restrictions varied across the nation. The South, Beale found, was most restrictive; the Northeast, the most permissive. In the Northeast, three-fifths of the teachers surveyed felt free to swear, and three-fifths thought that they would not be punished for gambling. Only a third of Southern teachers thought they would not be fired for gambling, and only one in thirty-five believed they could swear in the classroom.

But some taboos were nearly everywhere. A 1931 NEA survey reported that twenty-eight of the nation's ninety-three largest cities fired pregnant teachers. And Beale found one teacher from Oak Park, Illinois, who would not smoke in a train or hotel, even if she was 2000 miles away from her classroom, "because, well, someone from Oak Park might see her, and the Principal might not like it if he knew."[12]

These restrictions persisted in most of America throughout

the 1940s. When August Hollingshead studied the rural Illinois city he called Elmtown during 1941 and 1942, he observed that the high school teachers were required by the school board to live in the "good" sections of town, buy their goods from local merchants (who complained when teachers bought from chain stores), and "attend church, teach Sunday school classes, sing in the choir, act as youth leaders, and make annual pledges" to local charities. Teachers were strongly discouraged from socializing, smoking in public, or being "seen at a tavern or at a public dance."[13]

The courts frequently upheld these locally created rules. In 1939, for example, a Pennsylvania court ruled that a teacher could be fired for moonlighting in her husband's tavern, where she played pinball and served beer to customers. The judge declared that by tending bar, the teacher had lost the respect of the community and was incompetent to teach.

Teachers often found community strictures stifling. Indeed, conflicts between teachers and communities over moral issues were a popular plot in the fiction of the time. In Sophia Belzer Engstrand's 1940 novel *Miss Munday,* the heroine observes that she and her colleagues "are treated in a special way, like vestal virgins set aside by the community to keep up the strict morality that people don't always practice for themselves."[14]

The best teachers of the era not only willingly maintained good morals but inculcated them. Many prominent Americans born before 1945 credit a high school teacher with prodding them to success. In *Making It* (1967), Norman Podhoretz described a high school English teacher he called "Mrs. K." When Podhoretz met Mrs. K, he was a troubled teenager whose favorite attire was "a tee-shirt, tightly pegged pants, and a red satin jacket with the legend 'Cherokees S.A.C.' [social-athletic club] stitched in large white letters across the back." Mrs. K. introduced Podhoretz to the Frick and Metropolitan Museums, restaurants, and the theater, and nearly bought him his first suit. Although Podhoretz observed that Mrs. K had "astonishing rudeness," he credits her with helping to transform him from "looking and sounding like a 'filthy little slum child'" to becoming an urban sophisticate.[15]

While the best teachers of the 1940s may well have been

harsh, their actions—and their teaching—were remembered gratefully by their students. In his 1969 memoir *Chalk Dust on My Shoulder*, Charles Rousculp, a teacher in the Worthington, Ohio, high school, recalled a colleague named Jeanette Fry, who taught Latin and French at the school between 1930 and 1965. Fry's temper was legendary. If a student didn't turn in his or her homework or did the work badly, Fry would routinely put "on a display of pyrotechnics that could transform a homecoming queen or a football halfback into a blubbering wreck." One student told Rousculp that Fry had placed him in a "quivering panic" because "she got so mad at me yesterday I was afraid she'd hurt herself pounding on the desk." But while students were terrified of Fry in high school, they were grateful to her as adults for the moral and character-building lessons they learned. "Year after year," Rousculp noted, Fry's students returned to Worthington "to seek out the woman who had taught them discipline better than many of their parents."[16]

But by 1945, Jeanette Fry, Mrs. K., and teachers like them were anachronisms. Postwar cultural and social changes would ensure that these iron-willed women would find other careers or, if they stayed in the schools, would be severely restricted in their jobs.

The changes that permanently weakened teachers can be traced to 1939, when Charles Allan Prosser delivered the Inglis lectures at Harvard. Since his successful campaign to make vocational education part of the American high school, Prosser had become one of the more important educational pundits of his time. Like most of the progressive educators of the day, Prosser believed that the primary purpose of schools was to teach practical subjects rather than inspire students to learn. "Every subject taught in our secondary schools," Prosser wrote, "should be selected on its merits for its use value and not for its value as a credential for admission to college." In his opinion, "the practice of modern English" was more important than Chaucer; "the simple business knowledge needed by everybody" more vital than algebra.[17]

Prosser warned that if schools did not implement his practical curriculum, they would lose what little influence on the

70

student they already had. The more high school serves "merely as a required gathering place for those who attend without profit, the more it tends to become merely a custodian; the more it uses its stewardship as a means of reaching and serving its students with a kind of education that will be of most benefit, the more it tends to become an educational institution."[18]

Prosser's cure for American schools proved to be a popular one. In *Education for ALL American Youth* (1944), the National Education Association called for schools to develop practical courses; in 1945 and 1946, the U.S. Office of Education considered spending millions to devise national models for what came to be known as "life-adjustment education." (Due to budget cuts in 1947, these national courses were never designed.) Derided throughout the 1950s by such advocates of the "back-to-basics" movement as Mortimer Smith, Arthur Bestor, and Hyman Rickover, the progressive education movement was temporarily checked. But the movement made its lasting mark—the balance of power between teachers and students had begun to shift in favor of the students.

The massive growth in the size and number of high schools also meant that community standards would disappear. In a February 1962 poll by the NEA, only 1.6 percent of those surveyed said that these standards had "seriously restricted" their behavior.[19] As long as teachers did not commit any illegal activities, what they did outside the classroom was now purely their own affair. American high schools in 1965 were still, for the most part, sturdy temples of learning, but their pillars had developed serious cracks that would weaken further as the decade progressed.

In the early 1960s, high school teachers remained largely low-ranking members of the establishment. In a March 1963 NEA poll, 56.3 percent of those surveyed said they were either "conservative" or "tended to be conservative." (Among female high school teachers, 65 percent said they were conservative; only 52 percent of men thought they were on the right politically.)[20]

But the late 1960s brought in thousands of teachers who did not enter the profession by traditional routes. As Myron Brenton noted in *Whatever Happened to Teacher?* (1970), these new teachers were "mini-skirted swingers, Ivy league intellectuals, former cabdrivers, grandmothers, ex-businessmen, Black Panthers, John Birch types, Rotary Club rooters, aggressive pacifists."[21]

This new influx of nontraditional teachers had two lasting effects on the schools. First, public high school teaching was permanently transformed from a largely female profession into one where neither gender dominated. Women left teaching for other, higher-paying professions; men entered the field, largely to escape the draft. Second, many of the new teachers, fortified by reading John Holt or Jonathan Kozol, listening to Jefferson Airplane or Bob Dylan albums, or watching *To Sir With Love,* attempted to alter the schools radically. Their efforts (combined with the steady growth in regulations by states and central offices) ensured that the moral consensus used as a basis for school governance was largely destroyed. In its place was what Gerald Grant described as "a more impersonal legal-bureaucratic order."[22] The decisions teachers made were no longer based primarily on whether or not student behavior was right or wrong, good or bad, but on whether or not a student's action violated federal statutes and district regulations. Had Jeanette Fry survived in the schools until the 1970s, her outbursts may well have violated student-rights codes or child-abuse laws.

Faced with an increasingly bureaucratic workplace, a rising number of teachers were doing something unheard of by previous generations—they were "burning out" on the job. As Barry Farber, a professor of education and psychology at Teachers College, Columbia University, observed, the term "burnout" was not commonly used until the 1970s. (It was apparently first used by Graham Greene in his 1961 novel *A Burnt-Out Case.*) But in the early 1970s, such noted psychologists as Christina Maslach and Herbert Freudenberger began to notice an increasing number of social workers frustrated by their jobs and working conditions and exhibiting "burned out" symptoms.

Some signs of burnout were detected by Dan C. Lortie, a sociologist at the University of Chicago, in his 1975 work *Schoolteacher.* Studying Dade County, Florida, schools in the early 1970s, Lortie found that the teachers were largely dissatisfied with their work. Among teachers, Lortie wrote, "one finds self-blame, a sense of inadequacy, the bitter taste of failure, anger at the students, despair, and other dark emotions."[23]

In the teacher's world that Lortie described, most decisions were controlled by outsiders. Central offices mandated the supplies and curricula teachers used; textbooks were becoming "teacher-proof." There was no "chain of achievement" in a career; lawyers eventually made partner, assistant professors became tenured professors, but seasoned high school teachers remained just plain teachers.

"Good days," when a teacher felt that he or she did a good job, were rare, and usually occurred when a teacher was not interrupted by outsiders. Anyone who caused an interruption was at fault; "negative allusions were made to the parents, the principal, the school nurse, colleagues."[24] Thirty-four percent of the teachers Lortie surveyed said that "clerical duties" interfered with their work; 24 percent thought that administrators were more hindrance than help. Parents were seen by teachers as nuisances who constantly complained but rarely gave praise. Teacher autonomy, Lortie observed, was "informal, fragile (particularly when trouble occurs), and limited."[25]

Autonomy would decline further, Lortie predicted, as education—thanks to the Nixon administration's "New Federalist" revenue-sharing policies—increasingly became a matter for state rather than local government. If teachers were increasingly controlled by remote state boards of education, Lortie asked, would they think of themselves as "bureaucrats within the governing structure"?[26]

Lortie's prediction proved correct. As the 1970s progressed, schools became more bureaucratic, and a rising number of teachers fled to other, more satisfying jobs. During New York City's fiscal crisis in the mid-1970s, for example, one-quarter of the teachers who quit did not return, finding their new jobs as secretaries or bank tellers less stressful and safer than the classroom.

For those who remained, the classroom was becoming more dangerous and frustrating. To say that schools became more violent in the 1970s is too broad a generalization, since no reliable national statistics exist on classroom violence. But it's clear that during this decade, many teachers found schools to be a dangerous place in which to work. In the 1973/74 school year, for example, New York City schools reported 3,944 "incidents" in the classroom, including 1,434 assaults, forty-four sex offenses, 172 robberies, and ninety-five cases of weapon possession. A manual prepared by the United Federation of Teachers warned its New York City members not to arrive too early or too late, never to be in a classroom alone (including the faculty lounge), and to bolt down everything, particularly chairs, since "light, movable furniture is a recent favorite of younger children who are prone to throwing things at teachers."[27]

Concern over school violence continued to increase in the late 1970s. But in a 1978 survey from the National Institute of Education, 48 percent of the teachers polled said that students had insulted or made obscene gestures at them during the previous month. A 1979 poll from the New York State United Teachers asked teachers to list their ten most pressing problems; teacher–student relations accounted for four of them. (Disruptive students was the highest ranking problem; "maintaining self-control" was third, student verbal abuse ninth, and "theft and destruction of teacher property" tenth.)[28] By 1980, the city of Tacoma, Washington, was even selling teachers "stress insurance."

Salaries and work loads for America's public school teachers did steadily improve, however, with salaries rising from $22,800 in 1959 to $32,029 in 1989 (in constant 1989 dollars). The teachers of the 1980s were more specialized; teachers rarely had to teach courses in two unrelated subjects, as did their counterparts in the 1930s. But in many ways, the teacher's job had become considerably harder. The number of students who saw their high school teachers as symbols of authority—and respect—had substantially declined.

In a 1981 article in *Daedalus*, Alonzo A. Crim, at the time superintendent of Atlanta's public schools, summarized the findings of eighteen studies of teenagers conducted between 1954 and 1980. In 1960, according to these studies, teenagers were primarily influenced by their parents, teachers, their peers, ministers or rabbis, and youth club leaders (including coaches and scoutmasters). In 1980, the strongest influences on teenagers were their friends, their parents, the media (including television, music, and movies), teachers, and "popular heroes, idols in sports and music."[29]

Crim's findings were reflected in television and movies about high schools. The teachers depicted on such popular shows as "Our Miss Brooks" and "Mr. Novak" were characters who, although sometimes comic and occasionally befuddled, were always in command. In the 1980s, a rising number of teenage comedies, such as *Teachers* (1984) and *Ferris Bueller's Day Off* (1986) portrayed teachers as humorless buffoons whose only function was to prevent teenagers from having a good time.

Faced with a world where Madonna and Michael Jordan were more respected than whatever went on inside the classroom, many teachers gave up rather than attempt to alter student behavior. "Most of the time we'll all just play out the roles," a recently retired high school teacher told Barry Farber. "They'll come to class because they have to and most won't listen at all because they think that's the cool thing to do.... Most of the public thinks teachers are the villains in this, but you'd have to be superhuman to take the abuse we do every day and still care a lot."[30]

"The erosion of the social bases of authority has meant that schools are less pleasant places [in which] to teach and to work," says Gerald Grant, "and no one is more aware of the fact than students currently sitting in high school classrooms."[31]

In the 1980s, Charles Allan Prosser's prediction was proven wrong. Students were selecting courses based on their "use value," but as a result, standards were devalued, not preserved. High schools had largely become custodial institutions. Indeed, when Arthur Powell, Eleanor Farrar, and David K. Cohen surveyed fifteen high schools in four states during 1982 and 1983, they discovered striking resemblances between high schools and shopping malls.

Like malls, high schools had become temples of consumption where products were carefully marketed with "distinct features designed to appeal to a particular set of consumer tastes." In one high school Powell and his colleagues visited, sophomores could pick their English class based on whether or not they wanted to read two books a week, "read and write only when you have to," or do all homework during class time.[32]

Students who wanted a first-class education could obtain it, but few adults were willing to tell students what was right and what was wrong. The guidance counselors in shopping mall high schools spent most of their time keeping records. "On average," said Powell, "a counselor spent ten minutes with each student each year."[33] As long as a student's action did not break the law or involve violence, it was usually allowed. Punishment in many cases was light; in one high school, students were free to wear Walkmen during detention.

Indeed, many teachers went to extraordinary lengths to excuse student behavior. For example, in one large high school Powell's team visited, students were constantly vandalizing lockers. Rather than confront the students and tell them that destroying school property was wrong, teachers preferred "pragmatic, managerial solutions," such as hiring more school patrols. One teacher even argued that the problem was the result of "badly made" lockers, not the students who attacked them.[34]

Classes operated as a series of "treaties" between students and teachers, in which students were permitted a wide range of behavior in return for doing school work some of the time. In the shopping mall high school, classes were routinely interrupted by announcements, visits from counselors, and even students selling newspaper subscriptions. The most popular teachers were frequently those who yearned to be the student's friend. Students found one teacher particularly pleasing because of his frank discussions of his love life. "He's fun," a student told Powell. "You can bring donuts to class and chocolate-covered pretzels and all that sort of good stuff. We eat a lot in most of my classes."[35]

Moreover, the teachers who tried to make students work hard frequently had to face angry complaints from parents. Patrick Welsh, a high school English teacher in Alexandria, Virginia, reports that parents in his city have accosted teachers at seven in the morning, tried to have their normal students declared "learning disabled" on the grounds that a student "had to work hard to get good grades," and even threatened to complain to President George Bush if their child was expelled. According to Welsh, a former school board member in Alexandria managed to convince her colleagues to lower the city's grade point average for an honor student from 3.5 to 3.0; "everyone knew that she had a child with a 3.3 score."

"Just to fail a kid takes up so much paperwork that some teachers don't want to go through it," Charles County, Maryland, history teacher Pat Collins told Welsh. "If you don't contact the parent, give administrators notices in triplicate, have a conference with the student and follow a bunch of other procedures, the kid passes."[36]

The most telling indicator of the harm that shopping mall schools have caused is the decline in scores for the Scholastic Aptitude Test. In a provocative article in *The Public Interest*, Charles Murray of the American Enterprise Institute and Harvard psychologist R. J. Herrnstein contend that most of the standard explanations for the SAT decline are wrong; falling test scores were not due to having more blacks, women, or lower-income whites taking the test, but to two specific changes. First, the SAT became somewhat easier; a student taking the test in 1973 would receive an average score about ten points higher because of test changes. But more important, while the average student did about as well in 1990 as in 1960 "smart" students—the top 10 to 15 percent of all high school students—did badly. The percentage of students who scored over 700 on the verbal test, for example, fell by 40 percent from 1962 until the mid-1970s, a decline that has remained unaltered ever since. (A similar decline took place among students with 700-plus scores in mathematics; but unlike the verbal score drop, this decline has been reversed, suggesting that the problem is due to high school liberal arts courses rather than changes in math and science.)

Murray and Herrnstein suggest that this decline might well tie in with the shopping mall phenomenon. If no one is willing to push students to work hard and take challenging courses, they say, many students (like many adults) will choose to avoid work they do not have to perform. "There are plenty of students with high IQs who will happily choose to write about *The Hobbit* instead of *Pride and Prejudice* for a term paper if the option is given to them," the authors say. "Few of the most brilliant youngsters tackle the *Aeneid* on their own."[37]

The changes in American high schools that resulted from the "first wave" of school reform in 1983/84 did little to halt the trends that had turned high schools into shopping-mall-type institutions. In a 1988 survey for the Carnegie Foundation for the Advancement of Teaching, the Wirthlin Group polled 13,576 teachers on how reforms had affected their school. Students, the teachers reported, were more diligent than in 1983; 66 percent of the teachers surveyed said that student math scores had improved, and 64 percent said that their students were better writers. Nearly 58 percent of the teachers said they had more freedom to set the goals of their school, and 42 percent thought that the classroom was more orderly.

But in many ways, school reform had made the teacher's job more difficult. Over 57 percent of the teachers surveyed said that state regulation of their schools had increased, and 52 percent said that the "burden of bureaucratic paperwork" had risen. (In Texas, where the battles over school reform were particularly fierce, 80 percent of the teachers surveyed thought that regulation had increased, and 61 percent were more burdened by paperwork.) Nationally, 49 percent of the teachers polled thought that morale had declined as a result of school reform, 28 percent said there was no change, and only 23 percent thought that school reform had improved morale.[38]

A 1989 survey done by Gallup for Phi Delta Kappa partially supported the Wirthlin Group findings. School reform had not affected one fundamental problem of American schools—the unwillingness of many students to learn. Among the problems that teachers claimed happened "most of the time" or "fairly often" were students not finishing their homework (85 percent), truancy (67 percent), cheating (64 percent), skipping classes (59 percent), and "disruptive behavior" (50 percent). The three biggest problems schools faced, the teachers reported, were pupil disinterest and truancy (35 percent, up from 23 percent in 1984), lack of money (25 percent), and lack of parental interest (25 percent).

In the Gallup poll, teachers were asked to rank themselves on a "status scale" with other professions. The teachers thought they were still important; when asked to judge their profession on the basis of "the general good of society," teachers gave themselves an 8.8 on a one-to-ten scale, higher than the grade they gave clergy (8.4) or local political officeholders (5.8). But when asked to rank themselves in terms of prestige, the teachers placed themselves on the bottom of the status ladder. By giving themselves a 4.7 rating, teachers thought they had lower status than realtors (5.4), funeral directors (5.2), and advertising copy-writers (5.4).[39]

In the only major study of teachers conducted since the "first wave" of school reform, Susan Moore Johnson's *Teachers at Work* (1990), teachers' complaints were largely the same as before reforms were implemented. Surveying teachers in 1986/87, Johnson discovered that the public high school teachers she surveyed worked in a regimented, bureaucratic world. Less than 10 percent of the public high school teachers she studied thought "that they exerted ongoing influence over important schoolwide matters."[40]

While central offices, state, and federal bureaucrats were eager to create new rules for teachers to follow, teachers rarely saw or spoke to these out-of-school regulators. Many teachers thought that central office administrators "worked in a world apart, one untroubled by teachers' concerns and uninformed by their experience."[41]

Public school teachers, Johnson found, were rarely able to define why they were teachers or what their school's goals were. Most public high schools had lists of goals, but they were simply pieces of paper produced to satisfy evaluation regulations. "No teachers suggested that faculty were actually guided by them."[42]

Teachers were clear, however, on one point: the ways high schools are currently run had to change. "What we need in High School is 'Masterpiece Theatre,'" one high school teacher told Johnson. "What we have is 'Let's Make a Deal.'"[43]

But what steps should be taken to produce excellent high

schools? Consider these proposed reforms: raising teacher salaries and instituting national tests. As Johnson observed, raising teacher salaries or creating "career ladders" is not a solution to problems most teachers face every day. Well-paid teachers, she contends, would still have to face "professional isolation, large and impersonal schools, unproductive home/school relationships, trivial in-service training, and scarce recognition for good work."[44]

Advocates of national tests would do well to consider the experience states have had with tests in the wake of the 1983/85 school reforms. As *U.S. News and World Report* education editor Thomas Toch showed in *In the Name of Excellence,* schools predictably responded to the increased emphasis on test scores by requiring teachers to spend more time on tests and less time on the curriculum. In California, Toch discovered an eleventh-grade English curriculum that mandated that students spend 15 percent of their time preparing for the Scholastic Aptitude Test—and 10 percent of their time reading. (In Florida, a high school Toch visited even had a pep rally, where cheerleaders urged students to "catch that testing spirit . . .pass that test, pass that test, pass that test."[45])

Moreover, national testing is a prescriptive reform; advocates of such tests contend that if schools are required to have a certain percentage of students pass a test, they will somehow adapt their corporate culture to the new requirements. Yet it is unclear how this might happen. If the major problem teachers face is a remote and inflexible bureaucracy, how will imposing new requirements from Washington improve the teacher's workday?

Moreover, as Manpower Research Development Corporation senior associate Edward Pauly shows in *The Classroom Crucible* (1991), there is little evidence that any requirement imposed from above has any effect on what goes on in the classroom. This discovery is not new. When James S. Coleman and his associates surveyed American public schools in *Equality of Educational Opportunity* (1966), they could not find any educational policy or strategy that would successfully ensure student achievement.

In Coleman's wake, educational evaluators have tried to

produce a curriculum or policy that, when implemented, would ensure that students produce. Occasionally, a policy would get better results from students, but Pauly contended that this was due to what sociologists call the "Hawthorne effect"—that people, when told they are taking part in an important experiment, will temporarily alter their behavior to be more productive.[46] Accounting for the Hawthorne effect, Pauly concluded, "when the entire literature of evaluation studies from the 1960s through the mid-1980s is taken together, one finds no known policies that consistently improve student achievement—which is exactly what Coleman found."[47] Permissive policies (more counselors and other support staff) were as ineffectual in changing schools as tough ones.

Pauly's views are supported by some studies that come under what sociologists call "implementation research"—studies that show whether or not a new program or policy produces the results it was intended to produce. The most controversial of these implementation studies (known as the "Change Agent" study) was conducted between 1973 and 1978 by a RAND research team led by Paul Berman and Milbrey McLaughlin. The RAND researchers found that the amount of funding had no effect on whether a given educational program worked. The best indicator of whether a new program would produce lasting reforms in the school, RAND reported, was whether or not school systems could commit themselves to change.

Ten years later, McLaughlin (who had become a Stanford professor of education) reviewed the Change Agent study. While most of the recommendations of the study were still sound, McLaughlin thought that one point needed to be added: *teachers matter*. When teachers enthusiastically support a new program, McLaughlin believed, that program might have a chance; without teacher support no amount of funding, regulation, policy guidance, or memoranda could force teachers to accept a change they did not like.

"Policy success depends critically on two factors," McLaughlin wrote, "local capacity and will. Capacity, admittedly a difficult issue, is something that policy can address. Training can be offered. Dollars can be provided. Consultants can be engaged to supply missing expertise. But will, or the attitudes, motivation, and beliefs that underlie an implementor's response to a policy's goals or strategies, is less amenable to policy intervention."[48]

"Even an army of auditors," McLaughlin added, "would be unable to force compliance with *the spirit* of the law—which is what matters in the long run. District officials may be compelled to establish a parent involvement program consistent with mandated practices, for example, but mandates cannot require them to welcome parents and facilitate their participation."[49]

Pauly agrees with McLaughlin, but places even more importance on the individual ability of teachers to change policies imposed from above. In Pauly's opinion, the widely differing ways teachers confront classroom problems does not just give teachers a veto power on new policies but ensures that such policies cannot be implemented at all. Pauly believed that individual classrooms varied tremendously because of a process he called "reciprocal power."

The authority a teacher wields is considerably different from that which a general has over his troops or a chief executive officer has over her vice presidents. In a classroom, students constantly test a teacher (by taunts, abuse, or by slow learners who keep back the pace of the class) to check the limits of the teacher's authority. Given the differences in people's personalities, each class establishes its own bounds of acceptable and unacceptable behavior. Such compacts between teachers and students do not mean that teachers always have to surrender to students' demands. As Alfie Kohn observed in a recent *Phi Delta Kappan*, the best teachers establish discipline, not by appealing to authority or bureaucracy, but by explaining to students why rules are necessary before learning can begin. Permissive policies—"gold stars, smiley faces, trophies, certificates, high grades, extra recess time, candy, money, and even praise"—don't work, Kohn contended, because establishing a love for learning cannot be done by constantly providing prizes for good behavior. "Do rewards motivate students? Absolutely. They motivate students to get rewarded."[50]

Pauly believed that educational policies imposed from

above did not work because they failed to take into account the way classrooms worked. Faced with a policy they did not like, teachers frequently closed the classroom door and taught whatever they knew would be effective. "The differences among classrooms are too great, their memberships too divergent, and the process of classroom evolution too deeply rooted to be overcome by policy statements and official pronouncements."[51]

Instead of trying to find a way to fit teachers into a mold, Pauly suggested that schools might do well to adopt a reform implemented by schools in Newton, Massachusetts. There, parents, working with teachers and the principal, select the best classroom in a school for the students. By being free to select classrooms, parents become active partners in the high school, not isolated antagonists.

Another beneficial reform would be for central offices to devolve as much power as possible, either through school-based management or through school choice. It would be a major advance if central offices formulated their regulations on the assumption that teachers were competent unless proven otherwise. School bureaucracies currently act on the premise that teachers are incompetent and need to be governed, restricted, and ruled. The result has been a self-fulfilling prophecy: teachers, hampered by red tape and burdened by endless forms, have been far less effective than they would have been had they been left to their own devices. Allowing teachers, as much as possible, to exercise their independent initiative will do a great deal to improve American education.

NOTES

1. Cited in Louis A. Tucker, "A 1789 Teacher's Guide," *Boston Globe*, May 13, 1990.
2. Cited in Larry A. Cuban, *Teachers and Machines: The Classroom Use of Technology Since 1920* (New York: Teachers College Press, 1986), p. 4.
3. Cited in Myron C. Tuman, "Prometheus Bound: The Brief Teaching Careers of Great Writers," *Phi Delta Kappan*, December 1980.
4. Cited in Willard S. Elsbree, *The American Teacher: Evolution of a Profession in a Democracy* (New York: American Book Company, 1939), p. 297.
5. Gerald Grant, "The Teacher's Predicament," *Teachers College Record*, Spring 1983.
6. Robert S. Lynd & Helen Merrill Lynd, *Middletown: A Study in Contemporary American Culture* (New York: Harcourt, Brace,1929), pp. 193–194.
7. Ibid., p. 209.
8. Ibid., p. 210.
9. Arthur Powell, Eleanor Farrar, & David K. Cohen, *The Shopping Mall High School: Winners and Losers in the Educational Marketplace* (Boston: Houghton Mifflin, 1985), p. 240.
10. Frank E. Armbruster, *Our Children's Crippled Future: How American Education Has Failed* (New York: Quadrangle/New York Times, 1977), p. 79.
11. Cited in Howard K. Beale, *Are American Teachers Free? An Analysis of Restraints Upon the Freedom of Teaching in American Schools* (New York: Scribner's, 1936). p. 396.
12. Ibid., p. 377.
13. August B. Hollingshead, *Elmtown's Youth and Elmtown Revisited* (New York: Wiley, 1975), p. 94.
14. Sophia Belzer Engstrand, *Miss Munday: A Novel* (New York: Dial, 1940), p. 81.
15. Norman Podhoretz, *Making It* (New York: Random House, 1967), pp. 10–11.
16. Charles Rousculp, *Chalk Dust on My Shoulder* (Columbus, OH: Merrill, 1969), p. 43.
17. Charles Allen Prosser, *Secondary Education and Life* (Cambridge, MA: Harvard University Press, 1939), p. 9.

18. Ibid., pp. 84–85.
19. National Education Association. Research Division. *What Teachers Think: A Summary of Teacher Opinion Poll Findings, 1960–1965* (Washington, D.C.: National Education Association, 1965), p. 50.
20. Ibid., p. 51.
21. Myron Brenton, *Whatever Happened to Teacher?* (New York: Coward-McCann, 1970), p. 32.
22. Gerald Grant, *What We Learned at Hamilton High* (Cambridge, MA: Harvard University Press, 1988), p. 147.
23. Dan C. Lortie, *Schoolteacher: A Sociological Study* (Chicago: University of Chicago Press, 1975), p. 144.
24. Ibid., p. 169.
25. Ibid., p. 186.
26. Ibid., p. 227.
27. *Security in the Schools* (New York: United Federation of Teachers, 1974), p. 9.
28 Cited in Barry Farber, *Crisis in Education: Stress and Burnout in the American Teacher* (San Francisco: Jossey-Bass, 1991), p. 51.
29. Alonzo A. Crim, "A Community of Believers," *Daedalus*, Fall 1981, pp. 145–162.
30. Farber, op. cit., p. 122.
31. Grant, "Teacher's Predicament."
32. Powell, Farrar, & Cohen, *The Shopping Mall High School*, p. 21.
33. Ibid., p. 53.
34. Ibid., p. 56.
35. Ibid., p. 91.
36. Patrick Welsh, "Classroom Potatoes," *Washington Post*, May 24, 1992.
37. Charles Murray & R. J. Herrnstein, "What's Really Behind the SAT-Score Decline?", *The Public Interest*, Winter 1992.
38. *Report Card on School Reform: The Teachers Speak* (Princeton, NJ: Carnegie Foundation for the Advancement of Teaching, 1988), pp. 46–48.
39. Stanley Elam, *The Second Gallup/Phi Delta Kappa Survey of Public School Teacher Opinion: Portrait of a Beleaguered Profession* (Bloomington, IN: Phi Delta Kappa, 1989), p. 19.
40. Susan Moore Johnson, *Teachers at Work: Achieving Success in Our Schools* (New York: Basic Books, 1990), p. 191.
41. Ibid., p. 194.
42. Ibid., p. 229.
43. Ibid., p. 230.

44. Ibid., p. 57.
45. Thomas Toch, *In the Name of Excellence: The Struggle to Reform the Nation's Schools, Why It's Failing and What Should Be Done* (New York: Oxford University Press, 1991), p. 223.
46. The Hawthorne effect was named after experiments conducted by industrial psychologists Fritz Roethlisberger and Elton Mayo at Western Electric's Hawthorne, Illinois, plant between 1924 and 1936.
47. Edward Pauly, *The Classroom Crucible: What Really Works, What Doesn't, and Why* (New York: Basic Books, 1991), p. 25.
48. Milbrey Wallin McLaughlin, "Learning from Experience: Lessons from Policy Implementation," *Educational Evaluation and Policy Analysis,* Summer 1987, p. 172.
49. Ibid., p. 173.
50. Alfie Kohn, "Teaching Students to Care," *Phi Delta Kappan,* March 1991.
51. Pauly, op. cit., p. 92.

5

HOW
SCHOOLS
BECAME
CENTRALIZED

"To control a cow, you must make a large pasture."[1]
Zen proverb

*"The man who would be a superintendent of schools—
the educational leader of a city—must be clean, both in
person and mind; he must be temperate, both in speech and
act; he must be honest and square, and able to look men
straight in the eye; and he must be possessed of a high sense
of personal honor. . . . He must keep a level head, so as not to
be carried away by some new community enthusiasm, by
some clever political trick, or by the great discovery of some
wild-eyed reformer."*[2]
Ellwood P. Cubberley (1916)

By the early 1990s, it was clear that the bureaucratic structure that had governed American secondary schools for most of
the century had become unmanageable, ineffective, and costly.
In response, education reformers have pursued two strategies
for reducing the power of the central office. One is school choice.

The second would restructure the present system; it would transfer power from the central office to teachers, principals and, in some cases, parents.

School decentralization comprises several allied, but distinct, movements: school-based management nationally, the school councils in Chicago, the Minnesota charter schools, and the grant-maintained schools in England. Though these movements vary considerably in detail, their reforms usually involve transferring some authority over the budget and the power to hire and fire staff from central office administrators to the schools themselves. These reforms are quite popular with the public. In the 1991 Gallup poll on education, 76 percent of Americans surveyed said they favored "more say for principals and teachers" in the schools. When asked how schools should be governed, 79 percent supported rule by a council of parents, teachers, and principals. Only 11 percent supported the existing system of school board control.[3]

Can school decentralization transform American schools? Or are other measures needed? To determine the answer, one must begin by explaining how American public schools became centralized in the first place. For school-based management is not an innovation; if instituted, it would simply return American public schools to the practices they abandoned at the turn of the century.

Until 1900, most public schools were under local control. In 1890, the average state department of education had two employees, but nearly 500,000 local school board trustees hired and fired employees, determined curricula, and set budgets. In rural schools, time was set aside every Friday for "declamations," times when parents could visit the schools and talk with teachers about their child's progress.

In the cities, "ward boards" ensured that large numbers of parents would have a substantial say in school affairs. In Philadelphia, for example, 545 ward board members ensured that parents could broach an elected official about problems. "A ward board, or ward representative," historian Joseph M. Cronin observes, "could 'ask around' and talk with people about vacancies and about the particular problems faced in an individual school building."[4]

At the turn of the century, notes historian David Tyack, "there was 'school-based management' and community control to a degree unimaginable in today's schools. Local trustees and parents selected the teachers, supervised their work, and sometimes boarded them in their homes."[5]

But between 1900 and 1915, local control of schools was systematically destroyed as a result of the Progressive movement. The Progressives believed that government agencies should be governed, not by politicians beholden to special interests but by highly trained nonpartisan experts who would serve the public interest. Their creed was best expressed by Herman Metz, comptroller of New York City at the turn of the century. "The practical man knows *how*," Metz wrote. "The scientific man knows *why*. The expert knows *how and why*."[6]

Thus in city after city, the Progressives steadily worked to eliminate the ward boards and replace them with a single consolidated board with a few members. In many cases, particularly in New York City, the reformers tended to be middle- and upper-class whites wary of giving control of the schools to immigrants. The Progressives also believed that centralized control would ensure that schools would be immune from patronage. "If there are men who will not accept the office of trustee unless they can appoint teachers and employ tradesmen," said Nicholas Murray Butler, leader of New York City's school reformers (and later Columbia University president), "there are other citizens worthy of respect, who have no taste for the distribution of spoils but are interested in education."[7] Arguments for the democratization of schools, Butler contended, were as foolish as those for the "democratization of the treatment of appendicitis."[8]

Most of New York City's ward board members were not under control of Tammany Hall or anyone else. Forty percent of them were Republicans, and most had respectable occupations; according to Columbia University historian Diane Ravitch, "more than half were merchants; others were lawyers, doctors, judges, and bank officials."[9] These solid citizens campaigned vigorously for local control; school board consolidation was opposed by New York's mayor, nearly all the teachers, fifteen out of the twenty-one members of the city's Board of Education, and the 100,000 parents who signed the petitions. The ward boards, nonetheless, were abolished in 1896, and the school boards in Brooklyn, Queens, and Staten Island were also abandoned when these cities merged into New York in 1898.

After the ward boards were abandoned, New York Mayor Sylvanus Van Wyck warned that the reform would do more harm than good. School board consolidation, he declared, was "a radical move in the wrong direction [bound] to destroy all local interest . . . [and] practically exclude the people from all management of the schools."[10]

Despite Van Wyck's warning, the school board remained small. What happened in New York happened in other cities. In Philadelphia, the reformers were wealthy Republicans, such as Anthony J. Drexel, Justus C. Strawbridge, and John Wanamaker, whose names live on in the city's department stores and universities. These bluebloods, Mrs. Cornelius Stevenson assured the American Academy of Political and Social Science in an 1895 speech, supported school board consolidation even though they did not send their children to public schools. "The wealthier part of the ward," Mrs. Stevenson said, "has only a platonic interest in the public schools. Its members do not send their children to these schools, as under their present political management no parents will send their children to them if they can send them to better schools."[11]

But when the patricians took over Philadelphia's schools after the 1904 consolidation, they also created jobs for themselves. Historian William H. Issel notes that, when Philadelphia's ward boards were abolished in 1904, the 540 members of the ward boards included sixty-three citizens who were in the Social Register. When the Philadelphia Board of Public Education was created in 1905, its twenty-one members included sixteen who were in the Blue Book and four in the Social Register.

School board consolidation in Philadelphia, Issel notes, had another troubling result. The ward boards tended to create courses in response to what parents wanted; the newly consolidated board preferred to choose sources based on what was trendy or faddish. "Reform signaled the end of diversity in styles of instruction and the multiplicity of criteria of evaluation that had followed logically from curricula and supervision patterned according to norms rooted in the class, nationality, race, and religion of a ward," Issel wrote. "The new system brought curricula patterned according to the laws of school psychology, and a supervisory staff loyal to their superiors and, beyond them, to the national corps of professional educators."[12]

Not every school board consolidation was a consequence of a patrician revolt. In St. Louis, for example, school board consolidation did result in the removal of dozens of ward board members whose only interest in education was the business that the schools could provide to their firms. (The St. Louis school board's building committee, for example, was nicknamed "Contractor's Roost," because nearly all the committee's members received lavish contracts to supply the schools with boilers, paint, and buildings.) But the lawyers, businessmen, and physicians who occupied St. Louis school board seats after the city's 1897 consolidation, while not corrupt, cared little about the concerns of the people. As historian Selwyn K. Troen observed, the consolidated St. Louis school board's chief function was to let the superintendent have his way. "In contrast to the extensive deliberations of subcommittees and the full board" held before consolidation, Troen writes, "the reformed board's meetings lasted on average about an hour, and in some cases but twenty minutes, as the directors merely approved reports and recommendations that had been prepared and previously circulated by its officers."[13]

The St. Louis school board reform received national attention. Harvard president Charles W. Eliot said that the consolidated St. Louis board was a model all America should emulate. The deference and timidity of the consolidated St. Louis board, Eliot said, was to be expected; after all, school board members were "not specially qualified in the various departments of educational work," and should therefore follow the advice of professional educators.[14]

The swift process of school board consolidation had Chicago Teachers Union president Margaret Haley warning in 1909 that "our city school systems shall become great machines, in which one superintendent 'presses the button' and all the teachers move absolutely as he directs."[15]

Another prescient critic of school consolidation was Samuel T. Dutton, a professor of school administration at Columbia University's Teachers College. In his 1903 work *School Management*, Dutton predicted that "the efficacy of centralized school management, such as several large American cities have adopted, will be tested by the degree to which the superintendent succeeds in controlling the huge forces under his command without excessive red tape. If centralization of power should mean such a refinement of rules and such curtailment of individual freedom, and such exasperating espionage as to depress the spirits and cripple the free action of teachers, there would certainly be a reaction in favor of the earlier and more democratic methods" of school governance.[16]

As parents lost ground, superintendents gained control and power. Until 1900, a superintendent was largely considered to be a sort of "master teacher" for a school system, someone who would set standards and lead by example. Few superintendents had trained for the job; an 1899 survey by the *Journal of Education* reported that of the 113 superintendents surveyed, 58.2 percent only had bachelor's degrees (and only one—the superintendent of the Bangor, Maine, schools—was a woman).

The men who ran school systems at the turn of the century thought of themselves as moral leaders. When Stanford University historian David Tyack studied obituaries of superintendents who died in the years around 1900, he found certain words constantly re-occurring in the tributes: earnest, Christian character, perseverance, Puritan stock, New England tradition, true scholar. "Leadership in public administration was often seen as a calling similar to that of a church missionary," Tyack wrote. "Indeed, in teacher's institutes superintendents were sometimes as interested in converting to religion as in evangelizing for schooling. Their belief in an 'all-seeing eye'—that God witnessed all human behavior—invested even the commonplace with cosmic significance."[17]

Many of the turn-of-the century superintendents were iron-willed men. James M. Greenwood, superintendent of the Kansas City schools between 1874 and 1914, faithfully arrived at his office at seven in the morning every day for forty years, where he read Greek and parsed Latin verbs for two hours before beginning work. He died at his desk, a book in his hand. Others came to the schools from the churches. Anson Smyth, Toledo's first superintendent, had previously served as pastor of that city's First Congregational Church. Smyth believed that schools should not only teach "useful knowledge" but "what is of the highest possible importance, moral principles, order, decorum, truthfulness, purity, and virtue."[18]

But superintendents were soon to lose their spirituality. The superintendency became professionalized; from 1903 onwards, superintendents could obtain doctorates in educational administration either from Columbia University's Teachers College or from Stanford. But it took a second event to complete the transformation of superintendents into bureaucrats and the public schools into rigid, command-and-control bureaucracies: the "efficiency craze."

In the first years of the twentieth century, Frederick Winslow Taylor conducted a series of "time study" experiments showing that workers could vastly increase their productivity if their jobs were broken down into a series of easily repeatable acts. In 1910, lawyer Louis Brandeis (later a noted Supreme Court Justice) successfully argued before the Interstate Commerce Commission that a group of East Coast railroads should not be allowed to raise their rates because Taylor's research proved that the railroads could become more efficient without charging their customers more money.

A year later, Taylor summarized his research in *The Principles of Scientific Management* (1911). Taylor argued that any organization could be made more productive by using his methods. The principles of efficiency, Taylor wrote, "can be applied with equal force to all social activities: to the management of our homes; the management of our farms; the management of the business of our tradesmen, large and small; of our philanthropic institutions, our universities, and our governmental departments."[19] Taylor's book was widely popular and his ideas swiftly entered into general circulation.

Between 1910 and 1914, "efficiency experts" swarmed across factories, bureaucracies, churches, and even households and came up with ways to be more productive. (Their typical advice to mothers: serve standard meals at standard times.) By 1915, most organizations had forgotten the efficiency experts' advice. But not so the schools; the "efficiency craze" permanently altered the way they were run.

In 1912 and 1913, the *Ladies Home Journal* ran an eight-part investigation of American education and concluded that schools were largely failing to educate students. In New York, the *Journal* reported that winners of a *New York Times* essay contest were those who had the fewest composition classes, and that "the public librarians have shown that the most numerous requests for good literature come from those who have not studied literature in school."[20]

In San Francisco, Frederic Burk, president of the San Francisco State Normal School (now San Francisco State University), quizzed forty bright high school seniors in that city and found that only eleven out of forty could identify labor leader Samuel Gompers, while twenty-three of the forty did not know who Charles Darwin was. Some students, said Burk, thought that Booker T. Washington had assassinated Lincoln, that Sen. Robert LaFollette was "a Frenchman of the Fourteenth Century who explored," and that Charles Darwin had conspired to kill Mary, Queen of Scots.[21]

School superintendents, as Raymond Callahan shows in his *Education and the Cult of Efficiency* (1962), responded to public criticism in ways that resulted in permanent change. They began to pay more attention to items that could be *measured*—test scores, expenditures, salaries—and less to intangibles, such as determining what methods of instruction would best ensure that students would learn. Increasingly, also, these superintendents saw themselves more as chief executive officers of large corporations and less as scholars or professors. "Educational administrators," said Callahan, "by devoting more of their time and energy to the financial aspects of education and less to the instructional aspects, moved closer to the business-managerial role and away from the educational role."[22]

But how should schools become more efficient? Many different approaches were tried. In New York, Detroit, Boston, New Orleans, and elsewhere, efficiency bureaus were established. In Blackfoot, Idaho, the schools adopted "student efficiency tests," in which students were judged 2 percent more efficient if they slept with at least one window open and 5 percent more efficient if they made it a rule "to do a kindness toward someone each day."[23]

But the most lasting change was the brainstorm of a graduate student at Columbia University's Teachers College. For his doctoral dissertation, J. Howard Hutchinson studied various school systems to see how they managed their supplies and found that few could adequately describe how they ordered supplies or how many goods they had in stock. He recommended that schools adopt twenty-two forms, including purchase orders, time sheets, expense ledgers, and so on. Hutchinson's record-keeping was quite thorough; his form for ordering supplies and textbooks had nineteen entries, and his requisition forms had twenty-one (to be filled out in triplicate).

Hutchinson argued that, if his system was implemented, the public could be better informed about how school systems spent their tax dollars. "An inquisitive citizen could, from the accounting kept by [the] board of education, learn whether or not it was faithful to the trust imposed in it, i.e., whether it spent the money as it stated it did."[24] He also contended that his system would cost very little; school systems need only increase their budgets by $1,800 to pay for the cost of a clerk and his assistant.

Hutchinson's ideas spread rapidly throughout America. As David Tyack and Elizabeth Hansot show in *Managers of Virtue* (1982), most of America's educational leaders at the time were a close-knit group of men who went to the same graduate schools (usually Stanford or Columbia), frequently met at the same conferences, and whose careers routinely rotated between school superintendencies, high-ranking positions in the National Education Association and the U.S. Office of Education, foundation posts, and professorships at leading universities. Thus a dissertation, if published in the right place (such as Teachers College), could easily reach a select audience of people who could use the monograph's findings to make major changes in American education. As a result, by offering superintendents a relatively low-cost way to satisfy taxpayer demands for economy, Hutchinson's research proved far more influential than most graduate theses.

By 1920 the organization of American schools was firmly established. School districts were to have large central offices that restricted the autonomy of their schools by controlling supplies and regulating conduct and school governance. School superintendents, seeing themselves as the chief executives of institutions as complex as General Motors, created hierarchical management structures using organizational techniques (such as command-and-control or line-and-staff management) thought innovative at the time. Had these superintendents chosen alternative models of organization (such as those used in hospitals or churches), schools may well have emerged as decentralized institutions whose heads were considered scholars rather than bean counters. But this was not to happen.

The 1920s consolidated and made permanent the organizational trends instituted in previous decades. The graduate schools of education increasingly taught prospective superintendents that the legal and financial aspects of school administration were all that mattered. A survey conducted by John Sahlstrom for the American Historical Association in the 1933/34 school year reviewed eighteen major textbooks on school administration and found that 80 percent of the 8,196 pages reviewed were devoted to "the purely executive, organizational and legal aspects of administration."[25] And a 1931 study by the University of California's Axel Murphy asked school superintendents which courses were the most important; school finance and business administration ranked number one and two in the survey. (In last place: "education and the federal government.")

The power of school boards, denuded of parents and most concerned citizens, was drastically reduced. Stanford education professor Ellwood P. Cubberley, voicing the typical thinking of the era, called for school boards to include "men who are successful in the handling of large business undertakings—manufacturers, merchants, bankers, contractors, and professional men of large practice" and to exclude "inexperienced young men, men in minor business positions, and women."[26]

Cubberley's advice was largely followed, and the business leaders who ran the school boards deferred on most issues to the school superintendents. "The decline in popular participation in educational decision-making," says David Tyack, "gave local administrators greater autonomy in making regulations and exercising professional judgment."[27]

Vestiges of traditional standards and practices remained. A survey conducted by Frederick Haigh Bair in the 1931/32 school year for the American Historical Association asked 871 superintendents to describe themselves and their views. Most were white males; 62 percent could trace their family's origins in America to the year 1800. When asked about their fathers' occupations, 47.2 percent said they were the children of farmers; only fifty-five of the 871 were the children of educators (nine superintendents, forty-three teachers, and three professors). The two favorite books that these superintendents read in their youth were the Bible and *Pilgrim's Progress*. Two superintendents derived boyhood pleasure from Gibbon's *Decline and Fall of the Roman Empire;* another claimed his chief source of youthful delight was the *Congressional Record.*

Few of the pressure groups of today existed in 1931. Only 39 percent of the superintendents said that they were under any pressure at all, although, as Bair suggested, this may well have been because these men "have gone very carefully about avoiding any public offense."[28] Only ten said that any group asked to change the textbooks; only one was bothered by the media, complaining about "moron fodder that comes over radio." And few superintendents were inclined to revere politics or organizations devoted to social change. When asked which groups were "most important in advancing the country," the superintendents' three leading choices were the National Education Association, churches in general, and the Chamber of Commerce. Over twice as many superintendents thought that the Elks would do more for America than either the Democrats or the Republicans.

And at the height of the Depression, these superintendents were largely skeptical about making drastic changes. Sixty-four percent opposed government takeover of the railroads, 56 percent were against nationalizing hydroelectric power, and 79 percent disagreed with the statement that "our educational forces should be directed toward a more thoroughly socialistic order of society." However, 84 percent of the superintendents surveyed believed that history textbooks should omit facts "likely to arouse in the minds of students questions or doubt concerning the legitimacy of our social order and government."[29]

But if the values in which superintendents believed were slow to change, the school systems these superintendents ran were dramatically different organizations than a generation before. As schools became rigid bureaucracies, central offices began to grow, and the percentage of school budgets spent on teaching began to fall. Nowhere was this more evident than in Chicago, where the first major patronage scandal took place.

Patronage had been a minor embarrassment in the past. In his memoirs, Christopher A. "Boss" Buckley, who ran San Francisco's Republican machine between 1882 and 1891, recalled being startled one day when a newly hired teacher showed up in his office with a $250 "donation." "All the girls who are appointed pay you, don't they?" the teacher explained.[30]

But such conduct was unusual; given decentralized control of the schools, such scandals, when they happened, were mostly contained in one ward or district. The consolidation of power in a central office, however, ensured that there would be few curbs on that power if used unwisely. Such was the case in Chicago. When Republican William Hale "Big Bill" Thompson recaptured the Chicago mayoralty in 1927 (largely based on an unfulfilled promise to punch Britain's King George V "in the snoot" if elected), he promptly converted 3000 school jobs into patronage posts. When elections came around, the school janitors fled the classrooms and staffed the polling booths.

But although the Democrats, after returning to power in the 1931 elections, did abolish some corruption (such as closing mob-controlled speakeasies established in several high schools), Mayor Anton Cermak did little to reduce patronage. Indeed, says historian Mary J. Herrick, "the huge patronage payroll in the schools was much more important to the Democrats than it had ever been to Thompson. The Democrats made no attempt to reduce it—only to replace Republicans with Democrats."[31]

In 1933, Chicago schools faced a severe financial crisis. Hurt by the Depression and fed up with government, thousands of Chicagoans withheld their property taxes in a "tax strike." By 1933 the "strikers" had withheld $200 million in property taxes, monies that mostly went to pay for the school budget.

Faced with rising public criticism, Chicago's leading Democrats set a pattern faithfully followed by future generations: they fired teachers—and hired more administrators. While the Democrats busily fired 1,400 teachers (10 percent of the total), they added dozens of patronage jobs by hiring dozens of "lunchroom supervisors," a totally new position. As teachers were laid off, janitors and engineers received steady raises. By 1934, school engineers were making more money than principals, and "annually $370,000 more was spent on supervising, heating, and cleaning of school buildings than on directing the education of children."[32]

Admittedly, Chicago was an extreme case; in 1936, the Chicago schools spent 83 percent of their budget on administrators and support staff, compared to 35 percent in New York and 30 percent for Philadelphia. But the fact remains that in most cities the percentage of the school budget devoted to teaching continued to fall.

The school superintendency changed very little in the 1940s and 1950s. By 1950 the notion of the school superintendent as a scholar and innovator was in sharp decline. In the 1901 to 1910 period, reports historian Larry Cuban, 63 percent of school superintendents saw themselves as "teacher-scholars," 15 percent as chief administrators, and 13 percent as "negotiator-statesmen"; by the 1940s, the chief administrators rating had risen to 34 percent and that of "negotiator-statesmen" to 27 percent, while only 27 percent thought they were "teacher-scholars."[33]

But new social trends dramatically changed the school superintendent's job. First, the ramifications of the Supreme Court's *Brown* decisions in 1954 and 1955 ensured that, in many cities, the courts would play a major role in determining where children would go to school and what they would be taught. Second, the rise in teacher union membership and militancy from 1960 onwards meant that unions would be a major check on the superintendent's power. Third, the steady growth in federal spending on education beginning with the passage of the Elementary and Secondary Education Act in 1965 meant that a steadily rising percentage—and control—of a school system's budget would come from Washington or the state capital, not from local politicians.

These changes, says historian Keith Goldhammer, decreased the superintendent's independence; he became more of a diplomat and less of a commander. "The great problem for the school administrator was that he could not remain neutral in disputes between outside groups," Goldhammer writes. "Policy that would appease one group would antagonize another. Even failure to act was viewed as a commitment to one point of view and an instrument to be used by one group against another."[34]

In the late 1960s, many school districts became battle-grounds, as parents, teachers, students, the courts, and community activists fought for control. In many cases, the losers of a particular battle saw the central offices as rigid organizations unwilling to adapt to changing times. The addresses of central office headquarters—110 Livingston Street in New York City, 911 Locust in St. Louis, Pershing Road in Chicago—became synonyms for inflexibility and red tape.

If central offices were inflexible, some reformers asked, should they continue to exist? Were they necessary? Did schools need a massive bureaucracy at their core? This thinking led to the nation's first school decentralization experiments.

School decentralization was not a new idea. As early as 1940, Francois Cillié showed that decentralized school districts were better able to shift funds to low-income neighborhoods and help students with poor academic abilities than their centralized counterparts. But Cillié's work was forgotten; the prevailing wisdom in the 1940s and 1950s, expressed in such best-selling books as James Bryant Conant's The *American High School Today*

(1959), was that school districts should be consolidated to avoid wasteful duplication of resources.

The revival of school decentralization was largely due to the Ford Foundation. In the 1960s, the prevailing view at the foundation was that social programs designed to aid ghettoes would work better if the programs were decentralized and controlled as much as possible by poor people. Thus the foundation supported school decentralization with as much fervor as it backed tenant-managed public housing and early community development corporations.

New York City's schools in the mid-1960s were certainly in need of major reform. The central office was large and unwieldy; by some counts at the time, there were more educational administrators in New York City than in France. And as David Rogers showed in *110 Livingston Street* (1968), neither the school board nor the school superintendent could substantially change the system. The school board, Rogers reported, was appointed by the mayor, who made sure to include "three Protestants, three Catholics, and three Jews, a tradition referred to by one school official as 'the Noah's Ark principle of board selection.'"[35]

But the board was hampered in several ways. Board members who attempted to visit schools were routinely chastised by administrators who thought they lacked the professional credentials to adequately judge what they saw. The administrators preferred that board members act on the basis of reports by field supervisors. Under pressure from principals and district superintendents to make their schools "'look good' to their bureaucratic superiors," these supervisors "only reported on local school programs and conditions in a very selective way."[36] Unable to determine the true state of affairs in the schools and unwilling to acquire the power necessary to make changes, the board devoted its energies to minor issues; the cost of envelopes, for example, was a topic of great concern.

But the school superintendent also lacked power. The principals and district superintendents censored their reports to hide problems. His subordinates were bureaucrats with an "authoritarian and petty civil service outlook," more eager to enforce regulations than worry whether what they were doing was right or wrong. Any change the superintendent made was, in any case, usually blocked by a vengeful bureaucrat. No one—the superintendent, the board, or the administrators at 110 Livingston Street—could define the characteristics of a "good" principal, a "professional" performance on the job, or even what policies ensured good schools rather than bad ones.

Faced with these conditions, newly elected Mayor John Lindsay created a blue-ribbon panel led by former Johnson administration official McGeorge Bundy. The panel's report, issued in 1967, called for breaking up the New York schools into between thirty and sixty school districts. Parent assemblies would nominate six members of each district; the school system, five. Citywide licensing systems would, under this plan, have been abolished. But the districts, even after being broken up, would still be quite large; with between 12,000 and 40,000 pupils, they would be about the size of the school systems in Berkeley, California, or Evansville, Indiana.

In the same year, the Ford Foundation funded three demonstration projects to see if parents and community leaders could have a say in running the schools. At first the foundation thought that a governing board of parents and community leaders could control the schools, but under intense opposition from the United Federation of Teachers (UFT), who feared that a board would fire teachers or arbitrarily transfer teachers to ghetto schools, these boards were made purely advisory institutions with no power to hire or fire teachers.

In two of the three demonstration projects, the boards operated without incident. But the governing board in the Ocean Hill-Brownsville district was to be far more inflammatory. The Ocean Hill-Brownsville board acted on the premise that its members would eventually control the schools in their district. They did not believe in the art of compromise; the first principal they recommended hiring was Herman Ferguson, under indictment at the time for conspiring to assassinate civil rights leaders Roy Wilkins and Whitney Young. (He was subsequently convicted.) The UFT staged a one-day strike over the Ferguson nomination, and the governing board retaliated by saying that any striking teacher had resigned, and would have to be reviewed by a board "screening panel" before being rehired.

In the 1967/68 school year, the Ocean Hill-Brownsville board and the UFT kept raising the stakes. Much of the conflict can be traced to racial polarization; New York's schoolteachers were largely white, the community board black. But the board made a crucial mistake; it attacked its foes on the one issue (the power to hire and fire) about which teacher unions were (and are) least likely to compromise.

In April 1968, the Ocean Hill-Brownsville board "fired" nineteen teachers; the UFT held a short strike. Then during the summer of 1968, the board "fired" 350 teachers; the UFT struck at the beginning of the 1968/69 school year. The Board of Education ordered the teachers back to work and gave them police protection; angry parents and community activists stormed the police barricades, resulting in dozens of arrests. The UFT then struck for five weeks, one of the longest teacher strikes in American history. In November 1968, Lindsay decisively solved the crisis by abolishing the Ocean Hill-Brownsville and other community boards. Community control of schools was, for the time being, a dead issue.

Some commentators at the time, however, noted that the Ocean Hill-Brownsville conflict was but a symptom of the wider problem—the sclerotic, red-tape-ridden school bureaucracy that was the consequence of the Progressive drive towards school board consolidation. No commentator on the Ocean Hill-Brownsville affair was more prescient than Jason Epstein, later to become a top editor at Random House. "The effect of the impasse in New York City," Epstein wrote in a 1968 article in *The New York Review of Books*, "is that the monopolistic system is now incapable of performing even the minimal functions which have been routinely expected of it. It [the schools] cannot be trusted to keep the children off the streets and out of the parents' way nor can it continue to pretend that it is performing an educational service at all."[37]

In 1969, New York City school decentralization did eventuate, with several changes that substantially weakened the plan. High schools were not included in the plan; and while the thirty-two community school boards were given substantial power to control budgets, they could not set the curriculum or hire or fire teachers. (They had a limited power to hire principals.)

The new community school boards have helped New York City's schools somewhat. The schools became, in a small way, more adaptable and responsive to the problems of parents and concerned citizens. In a few cases (such as East Harlem's District 4), this flexibility allowed the schools to conduct the first experiments in public school choice.

But most of the time, community school boards have turned into patronage jobs for special interests. By 1973, the United Federation of Teachers had captured ninety-three of the 171 community school board seats. When David Rogers and Norman Y. Chung studied the new boards in *110 Livingston Street Revisited* (1983), they reported that, in most cases, community school board members were not parents or teachers but people backed by the teachers' union, political clubs, parochial school organizations, or antipoverty agencies.[38] A successful election to a community board could cost up to $20,000, making a campaign prohibitively expensive for parents unconnected to special interest groups.

Because few voters show up for community school board elections (the average is about 7 percent of eligible voters in a district), the boards have become a source of corruption, as board members divert the school budgets to cronies. In 1989, for example, ten board members in District 21 in southern Brooklyn had relatives on the city payrolls; these relatives, including the district's director of special education, a deputy superintendent, and an elementary school principal, were paid salaries of up to $60,000 annually by the city.[39] By late 1989, half of the city's community school boards were being investigated for corruption.

In his memoirs, former New York City school chancellor Joseph Fernandez contends that during his tenure as chancellor, between 1990 and 1993, many of the community boards were "being managed like Balkan states, playing 'let's make a deal' on every issue, standing for nothing (certainly not integrity), and systematically stifling what little faith there was in the educational process."[40] Here are some of the community board practices Fernandez described:

▶ Board 9, in the South Bronx, had hired a principal who was convicted of cocaine possession and a teacher who had been arrested for child molestation eight times. The board's president plead guilty to accepting a cashmere coat as a bribe and $18,000 in kickbacks from stationery suppliers. Three other members of the board plead guilty to charges of extortion, distributing illicit drugs, and stealing a piano; an executive assistant to the board once charged into the district superintendent's office with a gun and demanded that another executive assistant "step outside and die like a man."[41]

▶ Control of the school budget was so lax in Board 12 that teachers and supervisors routinely received pay for days that did not exist, such as February 30 and 31.

▶ Board 13 tried to reappoint a school principal convicted of stealing $20,000 in welfare funds.

▶ Board 17 hired a man named Henriot Zephirin to be the director of funded programs, a job that included buying textbooks. Zephirin gave a $46,000 contract to Luc Edouard to produce an introductory English textbook for French-speaking Haitian immigrants in the district. The textbook, reports Fernandez, "advises that 'earth' is pronounced 'erfe' and conjugated the verb 'chide' as 'chide, chid, chidden,' and 'catch' as 'catch, cought, cought.'"[42]

Zephirin was so impressed with Edouard's work that he bought 8,000 copies for the 100 French-speaking children in the district. Edouard said he returned $11,000 of his contract to Zephirin in cash in a parking lot. Zephirin subsequently purchased 2,000 copies of *The Red Badge of Courage* for 400 students who did not speak English; a cousin of his produced a twenty-one-page evaluation of the schools at a cost of $30,000, or $6 a word. The cousin said he kicked back $21,000 of the contract to Zephirin. Zephirin was subsequently convicted of grand larceny, falsifying documents, and defrauding the government.

New York City-style school decentralization was attempted in other cities but subsequently abandoned. Detroit schools, for example, were decentralized in 1971 and recentralized in 1980. And while large school districts would continue to claim they were decentralized and streamlined, a survey by Allan C. Ornstein in 1989 reported that only New York and St. Louis had more administrators outside the central office than inside. (Cleveland contended that its schools were decentralized, but the city had 258 administrators in the central office—and twelve in district offices.)[43]

In the 1970s and 1980s, central offices continued to expand steadily for two reasons. The first was the steady growth of federal regulation. Federal funds for public schools were never a major portion of school budgets. At their zenith, in the 1979/80 school year, federal funds accounted for 9.4 percent ($9.1 billion) of public elementary and secondary school budgets. By the 1990/91 school year (the most recent data available), federal spending for public elementary and secondary schools was 5.7 percent ($14.2 billion) of the total school budget.[44]

But the cost of administering federal funds—costs borne by states and local districts—was quite large. To ensure that federal dollars were wisely used, the creators of federal education programs demanded that fund recipients fill out innumerable forms. They also issued annoyingly precise regulations. In California, for example, federal regulators determined that the state could spend Title I funds on carpets only if sitting on the floor was part of a lesson plan. If students wanted to sit on the floor for fun, federal funds couldn't pay for the carpets. "The new regulations were rooted in mistrust of the motives and the capacity of local and school officials," observes David Kirp, a professor of public policy at the University of California (Berkeley).[45]

In the late 1960s, Mississippi education officials were caught diverting Title I funds for private gain. Congress responded by making even more stringent reporting requirements for subsequent federal aid, such as the Rehabilitation Act (1973) and the Education for the Handicapped Act (also known as Public Law 94-142, 1975). "We treated every state as if it were Mississippi," remarked Rep. Albert Quie (R—Minn.), a designer of many federal education programs.[46]

The result, notes Robert Kagan, a political scientist at the University of California (Berkeley), is that the many honest people who spent federal education funds well were being punished for the sins of the few cheaters. "Enforcers of criminal law require regular reports only from those on probation and parole," Kagan observes, "not from all citizens. In educational legislation, however, as in business regulation, when new abuses perpetrated by 'bad apples' (districts wholly indifferent or apathetic to the statutory goals), those requirements are imposed on all districts, including the reasonably 'good apples.'"[47]

But local school districts generated red tape on their own as well. David W. Seeley, an education professor at the College of Staten Island, noted that local schools created regulations as a cumbersome way to respond to complaints by parents or other concerned citizens. A problem with a teacher or a principal usually resulted in a system-wide regulation. If a student had a bad experience in a museum, the school district might restrict museum field trips. A parent who didn't like what Mr. Jones taught in his history class might have his complaint blossom into restrictions on what history teachers could teach. Each demand for change, said Seeley, resulted in more power—and more jobs—for the central office. "The greater the demands for accountability, the more securely the links in the chain of command are tightened, putting more power into the hands of those at the top and stifling the initiative and responsibility of those at the 'bottom.'"[48]

How much paperwork was generated by federal funds? The best estimate done so far is provided by John W. Meyer, a Stanford sociologist. In the 1976/77 school year, he reported, local dollars for schools created three times as many administrative positions as state funds. Federal education programs other than Title I were four and a half times as complex as state funds for schools. Title I funds were nineteen times as burdensome to administer as state education funds.[49]

Federal funds, moreover, resulted in administrators spending more time pushing paper and less observing schools. Princeton's Jane Hannaway studied school administrators overseeing federal education grants in a city of 500,000. These administrators spent 64 percent of their time in meetings and twice as much time pushing paper as other colleagues in the office. "The time-consuming administrative activities associated with federal programs are, at best, only marginally connected with what goes on in schools."[50]

Local districts and states, however, were certainly capable of generating bureaucracy on their own; in the 1983/85 wave of education reform, many states attempted to restore excellence to the classroom by regulation and micro-management. California mandated the amount of homework allowed; Texas and South Carolina ruled that classrooms could only be interrupted once a day with announcements.

But how could excellence be measured? Many states and school districts attempted to prove the excellence of their schools by quantifying data that could not be quantified. This had been an occasional bad habit of schools in the past; in 1926, for example, Chicago superintendent William McAndrew attempted to show the moral health of city classrooms by reporting that his students had performed 3,462,462 good deeds during "Clean Up Week." One unfortunate result of the excellence movement was that this occasional practice became a national bad habit.

In California, for example, teachers who wished to receive merit pay had to provide portfolios showing that they were superior teachers. These portfolios included photographs, journals, discussions with colleagues (known as "shared professional exchanges"), and "vivids," moments when the teacher did something special. "One state official who trains merit-pay 'evaluators,'" Theodore Hipple reported in *Education Week,* "suggested that a teacher could be 'vivid' by wearing an unusual hat to class."[51]

Judging and sorting through all the information collected in the name of "excellence," of course, meant more paperwork and more jobs for the central office. "Not only had some states hired people to monitor school reform, but there are cases of monitors monitoring the monitors," Thomas Timar and David L. Kirp wrote. "Those skeptical of state reform efforts see many of the reforms as a paper chase after meaningless data."[52]

By the late 1980s, the data schools collected were swamping

central offices. Some evidence suggests that all this information was unread and useless. In Ohio, the state legislature's Office of Education Oversight reported that during the 1989/90 school year a school district had to submit 330 forms to the Ohio Department of Education (ODE) totalling 1,094 pages. (With some optional programs, the total could rise to 479 forms.) So complex were these forms that many school districts had to ask the ODE to tell them what the data meant; some district super-intendents could not even determine how much money they were spending per student.

Much of the massive information the ODE collected was unused. In a fifty-eight-item form about handicapped children's use of school buses, the state used only two items; the transpor-tation division of ODE thought the remaining information had to be collected to satisfy federal special education regulations. (The ODE's special education office, unconsulted by the trans-portation department, reported that the information had not been required for eight years.) Another form about school buses had 437 items; the ODE only used fifty-three. The other informa-tion was collected because "ODE wants to encourage districts to keep detailed information on each bus, but does not believe the districts will do so unless they are required to report the infor-mation. ODE does not put this information into its computer."[53]

Still other information was unchecked. ODE required that districts submit the names and addresses of all students taking driver education classes before the state provided the districts with a subsidy. Although they checked to make sure that no addresses were duplicated, no attempt was made to verify that the students existed or were actually taking the course.

Thus federal, state, and local regulations and the natural impulses of bureaucracies combined to ensure the growth of central offices. In the 1949/50 school year, according to the National Center for Education Statistics, America's public ele-mentary and secondary schools employed 1.3 million people, of whom 914,000 (70.3 percent) were teachers. By 1969/70, the public schools hired 3.4 million people, of whom a little over 2 million (60.1 percent) were teachers. There were 4.6 million public school employees in the fall of 1991; and the 2.4 million teachers were 53 percent of the total.[54]

The 47 percent of public school employees not directly involved in educating children are ensuring that a substantial share of education spending is not reaching the classroom. The best recent analysis of the subject is provided by Bruce Cooper, a Fordham University education professor, and Robert Sarrel, a Fordham graduate student. They posed a simple question: How much of the 1988/89 New York City education budget was spent to educate children? The answer was not easy to find; Sarrel read the time sheets of 16,000 New York City Board of Education employees to find out how much time was actually spent teaching children. Cooper and Sarrel found that a good deal of cash cascaded through the system—but most of it was soaked up by administrators.

In the 1988/89 fiscal year, New York City spent about $1.6 billion to educate 268,495 high school students, at a cost of $6,107 per pupil. The board of education took 48.6 percent of this money for administrative costs, interest on debts, school buses, and security, granting $3,138 per pupil to the board's High School Division. The division then spent an additional $133 per pupil deciding how much money would go to each high school, leaving $3,005 per pupil (49.2 percent of the total) for the high schools themselves.

Administration costs within New York City high schools is also high. "Basic support"—librarians, counselors, psychologists, and teachers who prepared curricula or directed programs—consumed 4.9 percent ($299 per pupil) of the total school budget. Internal school administration, including the salaries of the principal, ten assistant principals, clerks, and secretaries, swallowed another 8.6 percent ($527 per pupil). The salaries of teachers who supervised other teachers took up another 3.4 percent ($207 per pupil). The amount left for the classroom: only $1,972 per pupil, or 32.3 percent of the budget.[55]

A somewhat similar analysis has been conducted by economist Robert Genetski for the Chicago schools. Genetski sought to compare costs in the 1989/90 school year between public schools in Chicago and comparable Catholic schools. In that school year, the public schools cost $5,548 per student, while the Catholic schools only cost $1,814 per student—and only charged $1,100 per student. (Church subsidies, fund raising, and endowments accounted for an additional $700 per student annually.) What accounted for the difference?

Public schools did have some expenditures that private schools did not have. Bus transportation is generally included in a public school budget and excluded from the private one. Genetski then subtracted all funds used for education of the handicapped and for bilingual education, and made an adjustment to account for the fact that, on average, only 82 percent of Chicago public school students show up for school each day. (Chicago parochial school students attend school, on average, 98 percent of the time.) These subtractions reduced the Chicago public school budget to $4,325 per student—or $3,682 if all special education funds were removed.

Genetski then added all conceivable costs to Catholic school budgets that he could find—$100 per student for textbooks, and $50 per student to ensure that priests and nuns were paid the same amount as lay teachers. But Chicago's Catholic schools paid teachers an average salary of $18,359, while the public schools in that city paid teachers an average of $38,409. If Chicago's Catholic school salaries were raised to public school levels, the cost per student would rise an additional $890 annually, or a maximum per student cost of $2,854.

After adjustments of private and public school data to improve comparability, Genetski noted that "the figures place the cost of private school in Chicago at anywhere from 45 to 77 percent of the cost of public education. A figure somewhere between these extremes is likely to be a fair representation of the difference between publicly run and privately run schools."[56]

The findings of Cooper and Genetski are not unusual. The Wisconsin Policy Research Institute's Douglas Munro has studied data sent to the Census Bureau by major school districts and notes that these districts told the Census that in the 1989/90 school year, between 30 and 60 percent of their budgets went to administrative expenses, not to classroom instruction. The cities that told the Census Bureau that they spent the most money on school administration were not limited to the decaying cities of the Northeast; while Washington, D.C., for example, said that 55.2 percent of its school budget went to administration, Phoenix, Arizona, said that its administrative expenses accounted for 56.4 percent of its school budget, while Broward County, Florida (which includes Fort Lauderdale), spent 57.9 percent of its school budget on administration.

But even these figures, says Munro, are misleading; Milwaukee, Wisconsin, for example, counts the money spent on caterers for meetings of the school administration. He believes a more accurate account of school spending is provided by the Indiana Policy Review Federation, which, in January 1993, reported that only 38 percent of Indiana state school spending (and 35.9 percent of Indianapolis city school spending) is spent in the classroom.[57]

With school organizations becoming large, complex, and unwieldy, school boards continued to decline in stature and importance. They continued to be burdened by state regulations that mandated that boards approve relatively trivial matters. West Virginia required school boards to approve all field trips; California insisted that boards ratify all student expulsions. In some cities, aided by low turnouts in elections, teachers unions began to elect their own members to school boards in substantial numbers. The United Teachers of Los Angeles elected four of its members to that city's school board in 1989; the board promptly instituted a rule that employees who were not members of the union should be required to pay union dues.

The leaders of school boards in the 1980s thought that their power had sharply declined. The National Center for Education Information surveyed school board presidents in 1988/89 and reported that 58 percent of the presidents surveyed thought their board's authority had declined, and 89 percent of these thought that the state board of education had increased control over their local board. While over 80 percent of the presidents said they were satisfied with their dealings with teachers, the superintendent, and parents, only 60 percent thought their relationship with the state board of education satisfactory.[58]

Thus hampered by unions, civil service regulations, or bureaucratic inertia, school boards responded to problems not by implementing substantive reforms but by firing the school superintendent.

Before the Progressive era, superintendents were regularly sacked to save money. One delegate to the 1879 convention revising the California state constitution even proposed that all state and county school superintendents be fired on the grounds that they were "mere parasites" who went to schools "asking some few silly questions."[59] By 1990, nearly a century's worth of effort to make the superintendent a strong, dominant commander had vanished; in many troubled districts, the superintendent had become the weakest player in the school system.

Superintendents have become the government equivalent of baseball managers. They are well paid. A 1990 survey by *Ebony* reports that the school superintendents of Chicago, Portland (Oregon), Dallas, and Baltimore were four of the ten highest paid black public officials in America. Chicago Superintendent Ted Kimbrough, with a salary of $175,000, earned far more than such better known black elected officials as Detroit Mayor Coleman Young, New York Mayor David Dinkins, or Virginia Governor Douglas Wilder.[60]

But the school superintendent's job is highly unstable; school boards usually respond to complaints by parents and teachers by firing the superintendent in the hope that a new leader will bring in a new management style and shake up the system. Patrick Welsh, a high school English teacher in Alexandria, Virginia, reported that between 1972 and 1990 the city had gone from "a public-relations conscious superintendent, to a hatchet man, then back to a consensus-builder, then [to] another tough house-cleaner."[61]

The constant rotation of the superintendent is quite costly. School boards not only have to spend money on headhunting, but the constant need for new superintendents ensures that cities can select from only a limited pool of talent. In early 1993, the Council of the Great City Schools reported that in forty out of the nation's forty-five largest school districts, the superintendent had held their jobs for less than three years. At that time, the nation's three largest school systems were looking for superintendents, New York's Joseph Fernandez and Chicago's Ted Kim-brough having been fired, while Los Angeles's William Anton had quit his post. America's fourth-biggest school district, Mi-ami, had gone through three superintendents in the three years since Joseph Fernandez left to become chancellor of the New York City schools. In December 1990, Boston, Detroit, Houston, Indianapolis, Kansas City, Milwaukee, St. Louis, and San Fran-cisco were all looking for superintendents.

Buying out the remainder of a contract is also expensive. In the 1990/91 school year, Cleveland spent $360,000 to get rid of its school superintendent; firing superintendent Joan Wilson cost Houston $425,000. When superintendent Edward J. Murphy retired from his Long Island, New York, school system in Sep-tember 1992, he received $100,000 in severance pay and was able to cash in unused annual and sick leave at a rate of $1,000 per day. Murphy's total severance package was worth over $900,000. In an unusual case, Boston's school board spent six months searching for a candidate; of the five finalists, a "black" candidate was found to be white, another candidate had been fired from his last post, and a third quit because of the board's constant feuding. Fed up with the school board's incompetence, Boston's City Council abolished the elected board and replaced it with one appointed by the mayor.[62]

But is changing the superintendent the only way a school system can be transformed? Or can public schools become de-centralized institutions that can easily adapt to change?

NOTES

1. Cited in Gary Sykes & Richard F. Elmore, "Making Schools Manageable: Policy and Administration for Tomorrow's Schools," in Jane Hannaway & Robert Crowson, eds., *The Politics of Reforming School Administration: The 1988 Yearbook of the Politics of Education Association* (Philadelphia: Falmer Press, 1989), p. 90.
2. Cited in Raymond F. Callahan, *Education and the Cult of Efficiency: A Study of the Social Forces that Shaped the Administration of the Public Schools* (Chicago: University of Chicago Press, 1962), p. 219.
3. See *Phi Delta Kappan*, September 1991.
4. Joseph M. Cronin, *The Control of Urban Schools: Perspective on the Power of Educational Reformers* (New York: Free Press, 1973), p. 57.
5. David Tyack, "'Restructuring' in Historical Perspective," *Teachers College Record*, Winter 1990, p. 176.
6. Cited in John D. Buecher & Edward R. Kantowicz, *Historical Dictionary of the Progressive Era, 1890–1920* (Westport, CN: Greenwood Press, 1988), p. 148.
7. Cited in Diane Ravitch, *The Great School Wars: A History of the New York Public Schools* (New York: Basic Books, 1974), p. 138.
8. Cited in David Seeley, *Education Through Partnership* (Washington, D.C.: American Enterprise Institute, 1985), p. 72.
9. Ravitch, op. cit., p. 152.
10. Cited in Francois Cillié, *Centralization or Decentralization? A Study in Educational Adaptation* (New York: Teachers College, Columbia University, 1940), p. 78.
11. William H. Issel, "Modernization in Philadelphia School Reform, 1882–1905," *Pennsylvania Magazine of History and Biography*, July 1970, p. 375.
12. Ibid.
13. Selwyn K. Troen, *The Public and the Schools: Shaping the St. Louis System, 1838–1920* (Columbia: University of Missouri Press, 1975), p. 218.
14. Ibid.
15. Cited in Cronin, op. cit., p. 59.
16. Samuel T. Dutton, *School Management: Practical Suggestions*

Concerning the Conduct and Life of the School (New York: Scribners, 1903), p. 75.

17. David Tyack, "Pilgrim's Progress: Toward a Social History of the School Superintendency, 1860–1960," *History of Education Quarterly*, Fall 1976.

18. Cited in William J. Reese, *Power and the Promise of School Reform: Grassroots Movements During the Progressive Era* (Boston: Routledge & Kegan Paul, 1986), p. 16.

19. Frederick Winslow Taylor, *The Principles of Scientific Management* (New York: Harper, 1911), p. 8.

20. William McAndrew, "The Danger of Running a Fool Factory," *Ladies Home Journal*, September 1912.

21. Frederic Burk, "Are We Living B.C. or A.D.?" *Ladies Home Journal*, September 1912.

22. Callahan, op. cit., p. 52.

23. Ibid., pp. 109–110.

24. J. Howard Hutchinson, *School Costs and School Accounting* (New York: Teachers College, Columbia University, 1914), p. 8.

25. Jesse H. Newlon, *Educational Administration as Social Policy* (New York: Scribner's, 1934), pp. 92–93.

26. Cited in L. Harmon Zeigler, Ellen Kehoe, & Jane Reisman, *City Managers and School Superintendents: Response to Community Conflict* (New York: Praeger, 1985), pp. 84–85.

27. Tyack, "Restructuring," p. 178.

28. Frederick Haigh Bair, *The Social Understandings of the Superintendent of Schools* (New York: Teachers College, Columbia University, 1934), p. 78.

29. Ibid., p. 65.

30. Cited in Paul E. Peterson, *The Politics of School Reform, 1870–1940* (Chicago: University of Chicago Press, 1985), pp. 80–81.

31. Mary J. Herrick, *The Chicago Schools: A Social and Political History* (Newbury Park, CA: Sage, 1971), p. 175. Thompson did, however, fire superintendent William McAndrew, whom he called "the King of England's stool pigeon."

32. Ibid., p. 219.

33. Larry Cuban, *Urban School Chiefs Under Fire* (Chicago: University of Chicago Press, 1976), p. 124.

34. Keith Goldhammer, "Roles of the American School Superintendent, 1954–1974," in Luvern L. Cunningham, Walter O. Hack, & Raphael O. Nystrom, eds., *Educational Administration:*

The Developing Decades (Berkeley, CA: McCutchan, 1977),
p. 155.

35. David Rogers, *110 Livingston Street: Politics and Bureaucracy in the New York City Schools* (New York: Random House, 1968),
p. 216.

36. Ibid., p. 231.

37. Jason Epstein, "The Brooklyn Dodgers," in Maurice R. Berube & Marilyn Gittell, eds., *Confrontation at Ocean Hill-Brownsville, The New York School Strikes of 1968* (New York: Praeger, 1969), p. 320. Epstein considered Milton Friedman's voucher plan to be "an interesting idea" but "unworldly and evidently suggested for polemical purposes."

38. David Rogers & Norman Y. Chung, *110 Livingston Street Revisited: Decentralization in Action* (New York: New York University Press, 1983), p. 217.

39. Leonard Buder, "Local Boards: A Failure to Reflect Schools," *New York Times*, February 16, 1989.

40. Joseph A. Fernandez with John Underwood, *Tales Out of School: Joseph Fernandez's Crusade to Rescue American Education* (Boston: Little Brown, 1993), p. 201.

41. Ibid., p. 202.

42. Ibid., p. 205.

43. Allan C. Ornstein, "Centralization and Decentralization of Large Public School Districts," *Urban Education*, July 1989.

44. National Center for Education Statistics, *Digest of Education Statistics 1993* (Washington, D.C.: U.S. Department of Education, 1993), p. 38.

45. David L. Kirp, introduction to Kirp and Donald N. Jensen, eds., *School Days, Rule Days: The Legalization and Regulation of Education* (Philadelphia: Falmer Press, 1986), p. 3.

46. Ibid., p. 3.

47. Robert A. Kagan, "Regulating Business, Regulating Schools: The Problem of Regulatory Unreasonableness," in Kirp and Jensen, op. cit., p. 79.

48. Seeley, op. cit., p. 42.

49. John W. Meyer, W. Richard Scott, & David Strong, "Centralization, Fragmentation, and School District Complexity," *Administrative Science Quarterly*, June 1987.

50. Jane Hannaway, "Administrative Costs and Administrative Behavior Associated with Categorical Programs," *Educational Evaluation and Policy Analysis*, Spring 1985, p. 62.

51. Cited in Thomas Timar & David L. Kirp, *Managing Educational Excellence* (Philadelphia: Falmer Press, 1988), p. 51.
52. Ibid., p. 113.
53. *Public School Reporting Requirements* (Columbus, OH: Legislative Office of Education Oversight, 1990), p. 17.
54. *Digest of Education Statistics 1993*, op. cit., p. 90.
55. Bruce S. Cooper & Robert Sarrel, "Managing for School Efficiency and Effectiveness: It Can be Done Even in New York City," *National Forum of Educational Administration and Supervision Journal*, v. 8, no. 3 (1991–92). See also Dana Wechsler, "Parkinson's Law 101," *Forbes*, June 25, 1990.
56. Robert Genetski, "Private Schools, Public Savings," *Wall Street Journal*, July 8, 1992.
57. Douglas P. Munro, *How to Find Out Where the Money Goes in the Public Schools*, (Washington, D.C.: Heritage Foundation, 1993).
58. C. Emily Feistritzer, *Profile of School Board Presidents in the U.S.* (Washington, D.C.: National Center for Education Information, 1989), p. 30.
59. Cited in David Tyack & Thomas James, "State Government and American Public Education: Exploring the 'Primeval Forest,'" *History of Education Quarterly*, Spring 1986.
60. "10 Highest Paid Black Officials," *Ebony*, September 1990.
61. Patrick Welsh, "A Lesson in Reading, Writing—and Red Tape," *Washington Post*, December 2, 1990.
62. Kenneth J. Cooper, "New School Superintendents Wanted in 17 Cities," *Washington Post*, December 16, 1990. Neal Pierce, "As Big Cities Lose, or Fire, School Superintendents, Vacancies Abound," syndicated column appearing in *Philadelphia Inquirer*, December 31, 1990. Chuck Sheperd & Jim Sweeney, "News of the Weird," *Washington City Paper*, February 12, 1993. Mary Jordan, "Big City School Chiefs Learn Reform Is Not 1 of the 3 Rs," *Washington Post*, February 12, 1993.

6

SCHOOL DECENTRALIZATION

School decentralization did not die in the flames of New York City's experimentation in the Ocean Hill-Brownsville district. It was clear that dividing school administrative functions into pieces did little to ensure lasting change. But it was also clear that central offices did not need many of their powers. Norman Drechler, a former Detroit school superintendent, notes that central office financial controls were particularly hard on principals. "We entrust to a principal the educational future of some three to four thousand students, a building often amounting to 10 or 15 million dollars," Drechler writes, "but we do not trust him or her with ten dollars worth of petty cash."[1]

Why not transfer some of the powers of the central office to schools? Why not give principals and teachers power to control their budgets and decide how their schools should be run? This sort of thinking led to what is now known generally as school restructuring, and more specifically as "school-based" or "site-based" management.

Like most ideas in American education, "school-based management" has very old roots. The first person to suggest transferring some power from the central offices to the schools was Ella Flagg Young, a leading figure in Chicago schools at the turn of the century. When she was a district superintendent of schools in 1898, Young created teacher councils in her district where teachers could gather and offer advice on problems to the superintendent. The councils were abolished the following year, but Young soon wrote a doctoral dissertation on the idea. Young thought that these teacher councils would ensure democracy in the schools. "The voice of authority of position not only must not dominate," Young wrote, "but must not be heard in the councils. . . . The membership of each school council should be small enough to make the decisions deliberate, not sensational. The necessity for such an organization that shall insure a free play of thought and its expression, rather than courage in opposing and declining . . . an not be made too emphatic."[2]

In 1913, when Young was Chicago's school superintendent, she restored the councils. They were abolished when Young retired in 1915, restored again in 1921, and abolished for good in 1924.

Superintendent William McAndrew had two reasons for abolishing the teacher councils. First, they met during the day, taking up valuable class time; but more important, such a council upset the hierarchy of the schools, and could therefore not be tolerated. "All stated works on school management," McAndrew wrote in a 1925 report, "repeat the obvious fact that in the fixing of responsibility, an orderly graduation of duties must be maintained, or chaos, confusion, and waste ensue. . . . Unless there can be shown benefits in the teaching unattainable through the regular organization, a return to the generally approved system is desirable."[3]

Teacher councils were occasionally created in other cities; such councils were created in Brooklyn in 1917, Fresno in 1926, and Cleveland in 1933. Some scholars of the 1930s wondered why the reform was not tried more often. "Unless Fascist principles gain supremacy over democratic traditions," Columbia University's Willard S. Elsbree wrote in 1939, "future teachers in America will play a much larger part in the planning and working out of public-school programs than have their pedagogical forebears. . . . The time is rapidly approaching when the old hierarchy which placed the teacher in a position subservient to that occupied by principals, supervisors, and administrators will disappear."[4]

But it took more than thirty years for the teacher council, under the new guise of school-based management, to reappear. The precise origins of school-based management are not known. Some scholars trace the idea to Edmonton, Alberta, others to Salt Lake City, still others to the University of Wisconsin (Milwaukee). The idea appears to have sprung up in several cities between 1973 and 1975. In the mid-1980s, several school districts, most notably Dade County, Florida, and Rochester, New York, adopted it; and school-based management is being tested in New York and Boston.

In most cases, a school-based management proposal means that school systems determine how much is spent per pupil, and then transfer some of this money to schools to spend as they desire. Usually a council of teachers and the principal (and, on occasion, parents) is created to oversee the school budget and to some extent control school policy. In most cases, some regulations are relaxed and central office pressure on schools is somewhat reduced.

A more precise definition of school-based management cannot be made. From the start, school restructuring has been a hazy sort of reform. Definitions of a "site-managed" or "restructured" school vary from state to state and even from district to district. "School restructuring has many of the characteristics of what political and organizational theorists call a 'garbage can,'" writes Harvard education professor Richard F. Elmore. "The theme of restructuring schools can accommodate a wide variety of conceptions about what is problematical about American education, as well as a wide variety of interest groups in search of problems."[5]

Thus the percentage of school funds transferred from central offices to schools varies. Teacher unions have, in some cases, insisted on enforcing all the terms of their contracts; thus some restructured schools do not have the power to add or subtract teachers, as unions insist that schools cannot increase the student-teacher ratio. School-based management policies thus must be judged on a case-to-case basis; the success or failure of school-based management in one district cannot be extrapolated nationally.

In some extreme cases, superintendents say they are going to introduce school-based management only to water down the proposal to preserve the status quo. In an article in *Phi Delta Kappan,* Kenneth A. Sirotnik of the University of Washington (Seattle) and Richard W. Clark of the Bellevue, Washington, schools tell of one school district where the superintendent declared that school-based management would be implemented, and that school staffs had to "focus their efforts" to make the reform succeed. "Therefore, he announced, the district staff would focus on improving instruction on language arts. Moreover, since language arts was a broad field, inservice training would focus on composition. In fact, since composition itself was such a broad area, the training would concentrate on the writing process. The inservice training specialist in each school would conduct faculty training sessions on October 21, January 15, and April 18. The superintendent concluded by assuring the principals that such school-based management would produce real improvements in instruction."[6]

This example may be an extreme case, but it illustrates a general point. School-based management is usually a reform imposed from above, introduced by school superintendents and school boards. And what is to prevent one superintendent from undoing or cancelling a reform instituted by his predecessor?

Some scholars argue that the top-down nature of school-based management reform ensures the ultimate failure of the idea. In *Politics, Markets, and America's Schools,* John Chubb and Terry Moe contend that school-based management, while better than the existing order, does little to change the bureaucratic nature of schools. School superintendents, they claim, fear bad schools, for these incite political opposition that leads to a superintendent being discredited or fired. To prevent failure and thus preserve their jobs, Chubb and Moe predict that superintendents will reinstitute regulations and controls, thus reducing or eliminating the benefits of school-based management. "School-based management, then, is another way of controlling the schools within an essentially bureaucratic system," Chubb and Moe

122

write. "Unless all goes well, then, there is a built-in tendency for decentralized systems to gravitate towards greater centralization. As long as higher authority exists, it will eventually get used."[7]

Chubb and Moe's scenario has yet to happen. While there are several cases of school-based management failure, these failures have so far not resulted in superintendents gaining control at the expense of teachers and principals. What is far more common is for principals and teachers to unite against parents, turning school-based management into little more than a PTA with a fancy name.

Consider the case of Salt Lake City. This city instituted school-based management in 1973. By 1988, school restructuring had evolved into a form similar to other cities. Each school had a School Improvement Council composed of teachers, administrators, and support staff and a School Community Council (SCC) made up of School Improvement Council members and parents. At least on paper the SCC had powers to control budgets, shape curricula, and help determine other school programs. In practice, report University of Utah researchers Betty Malen and Rodney T. Ogawa, SCCs systematically had their power checked or removed by principals and teachers. SCCs were routinely given an agenda determined by the School Improvement Council and told to approve it. In most SCC meetings, the principal led the discussion, set the agenda, and allowed little exchange of views. Whenever a substantive issue was introduced, such as the budget or staffing, SCC "members reported that they typically 'listen,' 'advise,' 'offer suggestions,' or take after-the-fact 'rubber-stamp, token action.'" In most cases, the principals and teachers limited parental involvement to holding fundraisers, discussing safety improvements, and determining when conferences between students and teachers were held.

The power of principals and teachers, Malen and Ogawa continued, ensured that school-based management in Salt Lake City "transformed policymaking bodies into auxiliary units, shifted teacher-parent parity to principal-professional control, and operated to maintain rather than alter traditional decision-making relationships at the site level."[8]

In a subsequent study, Malen, Ogawa, and Jennifer Kranz surveyed forty-four papers on school-based management. They first dismissed thirty-seven of the papers for being "advocacy pieces" that failed to analyze the reform objectively. The remaining seven studies showed no evidence that school-based management had any effect on school performance or student achievement. "There is little evidence that school-based management produces substantial or sustained improvements in either the attitudes of administrators and teachers or the instructional component of schools," Malen, Ogawa, and Kranz contended.[9]

For while many principals and teachers are eager to obtain autonomy from the central office, they are equally unwilling to let parents have a say in how they do their jobs. "To the teacher," historian Charles Glenn told *Teacher Magazine*, "the parent appears as an unpredictable and uncontrollable element—a force which endangers and may even destroy the existing authority system over which she has some measure of control."[10]

This fear of parents ensures that the primary beneficiaries of school-based management are principals and teachers. In Dade County, Florida, reporters first described the school-based management project there as a way of bringing parents into the process of school governance. "In an experiment intended to cut through red tape and create a new management model for large urban school districts," *New York Times* education writer Edward B. Fiske began in a 1988 front-page article, "the Dade County Public Schools have turned over the running of 32 schools to teams that include teachers and parents."[11]

Three years later, evaluators from the Dade County Public Schools's Office of Educational Accountability found that while teachers were largely satisfied with school-based management, parents saw no difference between schools where restructuring had taken place and schools where it had not. When parents with children in restructured schools were asked if "parents were treated with respect by the school," 62 percent said yes—the same percentage as parents with children in traditional schools. Moreover, while school-based management had resulted in a slight decline in dropout rates, there was no difference in test scores between children in restructured schools and children in traditional schools.[12]

In some cases, teachers and principals acquire some power to change schools and then refuse to use the power they have acquired due to the levels of bureaucracy that remain in the system. In *Reinventing the Schools* (1992), Steven F. Wilson of the Pioneer Institute reported that when Boston implemented school-based management in the 1990/91 school year all requests by principals and teachers to waive rules had to be approved by the city's school-based management steering committee, a school-based management central committee (a separate organization), the executive board of the city's teacher union, and the union membership as a whole.

Given the burdens of submitting waivers, few requests took place. In the 1990/91 school year, only twenty-nine requests were received. Of these, twenty-one were approved, and most of these requests were simple ones (such as changing a form or excusing students from taking part in a spelling bee). Two more requests were determined to be allowable under union rules. The remaining six requests were postponed indefinitely. All of the requests that were tabled, Wilson reports, "involved a union or the district demonstrating flexibility beyond granting an exception for a single staff member."[13] Similar results appear to have occurred in New York City, where the city's Chancellor of Schools, Joseph A. Fernandez, obtained his position largely as a result of the school-based management program he implemented as Superintendent of the Dade County, Florida, schools. When Fernandez announced a school-based management plan in New York in 1990, the city's newspapers were, at first, filled with stories with headlines reading "BLUNT NEW CHANCELLOR SHAKES UP BUREAUCRACIES."

But as Stephanie Gutmann reports in *NY: The City Journal*, the major beneficiaries in New York's school-based management reform appear to have been the United Federation of Teachers. School-based management, says Gutmann, is a "union job-generator." Union members not only get extra pay for training, but each school can receive up to $20,000 to implement the plan—money largely controlled by the union. The city has hired dozens of teachers to act as "facilitators" to ensure that school-based management is effective. Each new facilitator, Gutmann reports, is "sent away for several weeks of intensive training in facilitating at certified institutes of facilitation—with training paid for by the Board of Education."[14]

School-based management, Gutmann observes, is unlikely to produce lasting reforms in New York City's schools for two reasons—union dominance, and the veto power retained by the central office over school decisions. School-based management, she charges, "postpones the kind of dramatic reform that the New York City school system so drastically needs."[15]

The failure of school-based management in New York and Miami to produce lasting change does not mean, however, that it is a useless reform, only that it should be judged carefully. Mary Anne Raywid, an education professor at Hofstra University, suggests two tests for determining whether school-based management offers lasting change. First, do the newly formulated school councils advise the principal, or do they set school policy? Second, who has the power to hire the principal—the council or the superintendent? These questions, Raywid says, should be decisively answered before school-based management is implemented; too often, she writes, advocates of school restructuring "give no hint of intent to redress present power imbalances or to establish a new balance between school, district, and state levels of control."[16]

A recent report by the RAND Corporation offers a third test. For school-based management to succeed, say RAND researchers Paul T. Hill and Josephine Bonan, school superintendents have to commit themselves decisively to the reform. Districts where the superintendent suffers from "projectitis," weakly supporting several reforms at the same time, ensures that school-based management will fail. School-based management also cannot work, RAND says, when superintendents (such as those in Los Angeles and Montgomery County, Maryland) introduce the reform in a few schools and then withdraw it when test scores fail to improve. "Site-based management cannot succeed if it is regarded as one among many projects whereby the board and central office tinker with the schools," Hill and Bonan write. "When decentralization is seen as a purely experimental effort, teachers and principals are understandably reluctant to deviate from standard procedures."[17]

School-based management has not, so far, been instituted on a permanent basis anywhere in the United States. But a similar reform has been instituted in Great Britain. During the administration of Margaret Thatcher, British high schools, in some ways, became more centralized. Control of the school curriculum, for example, was taken away from borough councils and given to the Department of Education and Science. But the Education Reform Act of 1988 took two important steps towards eliminating school bureaucracy. First, local management of schools was established: state high schools were given control of 85 percent of their school budgets. Second, schools that met certain criteria could assume total control of their budgets, and thus "opt out" of the system.

To become a "grant maintained" high school requires the following steps. A school must create a board of governors and survey parents to discover if they want to opt out. If 20 percent of the parents sign a petition, or if the board decides to do so on its own, an election is held among the parents. If a majority of parents vote to opt out, a proposal is prepared for the Department for Education. The Secretary of State for Education and Science must then give his assent before a school becomes grant-maintained.

A grant-maintained school receives its entire budget from the Department for Education. Grant-maintained schools are still required to administer the national curriculum and national tests. And they cannot change teacher salaries, but they are free to hire as many teachers as they like. They can also spend their budgets as they please, subject to audit by the Department for Education. Grant-maintained schools cannot charge fees, but do have control over which students will be admitted. Their counterpart to our private schools cannot become grant-maintained, although they accept state funds under "voluntary-aided" programs (such as are given to most Catholic schools in Britain).[18]

Relatively few schools so far have become grant-maintained. Those that have report that they relish the freedom they have received. Grant-maintained schools have taken the funds formerly given as central office overhead (usually amounting to 25 percent of a school's budget) and used those funds to buy computers and better textbooks, and to hire more teachers. School headmasters also are pleased at the reduced red tape. John McIntosh of the London Oratory School says that school repairs formerly took up to three years; after opting out, many of the repairs have taken place the following day. "Once a decision is made, those involved in making the decision are here," McIntosh told the *Wall Street Journal*'s David Brooks. "We don't have a paper chase around the local education council for months."[19]

But other grant-maintained schools have had to overcome tremendous obstacles from local education agencies unwilling to see schools, and funds, cast loose from their control. When the Stratford School in London opted out, the local council seized the school's pianos, Venetian blinds, curtains, and even cleaning supplies. Some teachers forced students to write letters opposing the change to grant-maintained status.[20]

Grant-maintained schools, however, may be a fragile reform. The Labour Party has declared that the reform will be abolished if Labour returns to power. Some Labour-controlled city councils have also voted to block grant-maintained schools from buying janitorial or meal services used by other state schools. It is also unclear how much of a marketplace grant-maintained schools can create when they are required to offer the same curriculum as state schools.

It may well be that local management of schools will be a more lasting reform. For the choice British state high schools now have is not between complete regulation and total independence, but between controlling 85 percent and 100 percent of their budgets. Quite likely, a school used to allocating 85 percent of its budget will be more willing to sever all ties with higher rungs of authority than a school that has always been under central office control.

Some evidence that local management of schools is improving British education is offered by Her Majesty's Inspectorate (HMI), an independent government agency whose inspectors have judged the performance of British schools since 1839. In a recent report, the Senior Chief Inspector of Schools observes that the introduction of both grant-maintained schools and local management of schools has been generally successful. "Almost all schools welcomed financial delegation," the senior Chief Inspector noted. "In some schools, senior management has been revitalised by Local Management of Schools and the possibilities it has opened up." Grant-maintained schools, the Senior Chief Inspector added, "are now a firmly established part of educational provision. Standards of work in grant-maintained schools were rather higher than those in the maintained sector as a whole."[21] The Senior Chief Inspector reported that problems, however, still remained, principally based on the increasing burdens of time, energy, and paperwork that local management of schools placed on school governors.

The findings of Her Majesty's Inspectorate are most important both because of the organization's independence and because of HMI's traditional skepticism towards educational reforms. The qualified endorsement that HMI gives to programs that devolve power in schools suggest that these reforms are indeed beneficial.

While no American school system has implemented English-style opting out, one state and one city have come close. In June 1991, the Minnesota state legislature passed a bill, subsequently signed into law, that authorized the creation in the 1991/92 school year of up to eight "charter" or "outcome-based" schools.

Charter schools have more significant restrictions on their formation than grant-maintained schools. They can only be created by teachers, who will institute a nonprofit or cooperative organization to run a school. The distinction is significant; teachers in a cooperative are not part of a union, since they work for themselves, while teachers in a nonprofit school will still be union members, although they will form their own local branch.

Once the teachers decide to break away from the school system, they must institute a board of directors of parents and school staff who will in turn petition the state board of education for a charter. The state board then will create an advisory committee of ten members. (By law, two must be American Indians, two African American, two "Asian Pacific American," and two Hispanic; half must live inside the Minneapolis-St. Paul metropolitan area, half outside.) If the advisory committee approves the application, a charter school is created.

Charter schools cannot charge tuition, cannot be affiliated with a religious institution, have to accept all students who apply, and must comply with local zoning ordinances and state affirmative action laws. They are exempted from all other state laws and central office decrees. By law, each charter school is its own school district; it receives state and federal funds on the same basis as large multischool districts. Charters are to be reauthorized every three years.

The Minnesota chartered school initiative was a bipartisan effort. Though supported by Republican Governor Arne Carlson and Republican Senator David Durenburger, its chief backers in the state legislature are Democrats; the principal sponsor, State Senator Ember Reichsgott, thought up the idea after listening to American Federation of Teachers President Albert Shanker give a speech in 1988 calling for teachers to create their own schools. At first Senator Reichsgott proposed that any nonsectarian organization could create a charter school and that any public body could authorize a charter. But fierce opposition from the state chapters of the National Education Association and the American Federation of Teachers, as well as the Minnesota School Boards Association, led to restrictions on the number of charter schools and on the chartering process. Even after the restrictions were instituted, a motion introduced in the Minnesota House of Representatives to cancel charter schools failed by only four votes.

State Senator Reichsgott has made clear that the charter schools program will not be a prelude to private school choice. Charter schools, she told *Education Week*, were "not, in fact, the nose in the tent to the voucher system" but an alternative "that provides expansion of public-school choice without diverting dollars to private sectarian schools."[22]

It is too early to tell whether or not the charter schools movement will succeed; the first charter was given to a Montessori school in Winona, Minnesota, in December 1991, and it began operations in 1992.

In September 1992, California became the second state to pass charter school legislation. The California State Senate and Assembly were presented with two bills for charter schools, one introduced by state Senator Gary Hart, the other by state Assemblywoman Delain Eastin, both Democrats. Assemblywoman Eastin's bill would have allowed creation of 100 charter schools, required 60 percent of the charters granted to be given to low-performing schools, barred charter schools from restricting admission based on intellectual or athletic ability, and limited admission to a charter school to the boundaries of a sponsoring district. In addition, a charter had to be approved by 50 percent of the union members at a given school before the application was processed. Assemblywoman Eastin's bill was endorsed by the California Teachers Association.

Senator Hart's bill had none of these restrictions. The California state legislature could not reconcile the differences between the two bills, so they passed both measures. Republican Governor Pete Wilson vetoed Assemblywoman Eastin's bill and approved Senator Hart's bill, which became law in September 1992.

Under Sen. Hart's bill, a school district can authorize a charter school after it receives a petition from 10 percent of the teachers in the district or 50 percent of the teachers at any given school. Each petition has to, among other things, describe how the newly chartered school "is attempting to educate, what it means to be an educated person in the 21st century, and how learning best occurs." It also must show how the pupils in the school will become self-motivated, competent, and lifelong learners."[23] The school district then appoints a review board that grants or denies the petition. Once approved, a charter is granted for a five-year period.

It is far too early to tell if charter schools will be a success in California, but some districts are eagerly embracing the idea. Schools around the state, from rich suburbs to isolated small towns to urban ghettos, have applied for charters. By May 1993, twelve charters had been granted in California for the 1993/94 school year, including three in Los Angeles. While most of these charters are for elementary schools, the City of San Carlos plans to establish the first charter high school, complete with the provision that "each student who graduates from the San Carlos Charter High School will go on to attend a four-year college."[24]

Charter school legislation has been passed in California and Minnesota, and at least seven other states are considering establishment of charter schools. But other forms of school decentralization are also being tried.

America's largest exercise in school decentralization remains the Chicago system of school councils. Chicago's schools in the mid-1980s were in sorry shape. For years, the schools had hired weak superintendents, alternating between what leading Chicago school reformer G. Alfred Hess, Jr., described as "caretaker insiders and flamboyant, but ineffective, outsiders."[25] A 1984 survey of low-income high schools by the group Designs for Change reported that 49 percent of the students in these high schools dropped out and 53 percent of those that remained were functionally illiterate; only 4 percent of the graduated students could read at or above the national average. Chicago school spending, moreover, increased from $719 million in 1971 to $2.5 billion in 1991, even though enrollment fell 25 percent during this period.

The schools were also mired in red tape. In ghetto schools, the classroom period was cut from one hour to forty minutes on the grounds that low-income students could not keep still for an entire hour. In many of these schools, study halls were instituted during the first and last periods, allowing students to enter late and leave early. Principals could only be fired if they were convicted of a felony; at least one principal used the protection of tenure to leave school routinely for the golf course.

From 1986 on, a group of parents and community activists organized for reforms. At first the reformers called for schools to be decentralized in a manner similar to New York City's failed effort of the 1960s. But in 1987 and 1988, a nineteen-day teachers' strike, the unexpected death of Mayor Harold Washington, and the declaration by Secretary of Education William Bennett that Chicago's schools were not only "the worst in America" but in a state of "educational meltdown" ensured that more dramatic change would take place.

In 1988, the Illinois state legislature passed a law that created 542 local school councils in Chicago, each composed of six parents, two teachers, two community representatives, and the principal. To prevent a takeover by teachers unions and special interests, parents had six votes for local council members, and nonparents two, but the Illinois Supreme Court declared this voting method unconstitutional in December 1990; now, both parents and nonparents cast five votes for council members.

In Chicago, the local school council's chief power is to hire the principal. Principal tenure was, furthermore, abolished; all principals were given four-year contracts. The school councils also have authority to budget some state and federal funds for Chicago schools, chiefly money formerly used to implement desegregation policies, as well as a block grant provided by the Central Board of Education. But school councils have no power to hire or fire teachers, no control over curriculum, and very little control over unionized workers such as janitors and cafeteria employees.

The Chicago school reform has done some good. About 20 percent of the principals were fired as well as hundreds of central office administrators at Pershing Road. (Estimates range from 600 to 1,500 firings.) But in many ways, very little has changed.

The school bureaucracy has proven a formidable barrier to reform. At first, Pershing Road decreed that the councils could only meet twice a year due to budget cuts and could not meet at night due to the high costs of overtime they would have to pay school engineers. After this decision was reversed, Pershing Road and the councils warred over security forces; after months of wrangling, they declared that the schools would pay for police and the school councils would pay for extra guards. Pershing Road also was of little help to school councils seeking new principals or advice. "The last place many [school council] members could turn to for assistance or information was the central office," report Stephen K. Clements and Chester E. Finn, Jr. "Those who did call were frequently bounced from office to office and never did get usable answers to their questions."[26]

Pershing Road found time to spend $22 million, however, to refurbish their offices.

A second problem has been the inability of many local school councils to come up with constructive ways to improve the schools. Bureaucratic roadblocks and bad advice from school reformers have led to school councils simply repeating what has been said—and tried—before. Many improvement plans proposed by school councils, wrote William Ayers, an assistant professor of education at the University of Illinois (Chicago), "fall back on the taken-for-granted and the commonplace; they propose things like higher test scores, less truancy, and so on. . . . [I]f the schools do not break with their tradition of failure, then failure will be their constant companion."[27] "Probably 80 percent of the schools are status quo, 5 percent are worse off, and 15 percent are really going," Mike Smith, codirector of the Institute for Community Development, told *National Journal.*[28]

Unions also have done their part to block school reform. Teacher unions continue to insist on hefty raises; in the 1990/91 school year, Chicago paid for $71 million in teacher salary hikes by taking $66 million from the maintenance budget. (The *Chicago Sun-Times* reports that two-thirds of Chicago's school buildings are in "dire" need of repair.) Other unions do what they can to block change. Under the current contract, for example, each school still has one full-time firefighter, even though only five high-pressure boilers remain in city schools. Would these firefighters keep their jobs if a school council completely controlled budgets?

The Chicago school council program is a work in progress; it is too early to judge whether the policy is a success or a failure. But interest in joining school councils is declining. In 1989, 17,256 candidates competed for about 5,000 seats. In October 1991, only 8,196 candidates competed for the same 5,000 seats. In 1989, three candidates fought for every school council seat; and in 1991, one-quarter of the seats were uncontested.

Some commentators believe that school choice may be the only way to ensure that Chicago schools can be successfully reformed. "Decentralization by itself is not a panacea," observed *The Economist.* "Unless exposed to competition—and the real prospect of extinction—a public school, like any public monopoly, is bound to be careless of its customers' needs."[29] The *Economist*'s judgment is supported by many parents; a December 1990 poll by Northern Illinois University reports that 62 percent of Chicago residents favored public school choice, while 56 percent supported vouchers.[30] But in the summer of 1991 the Illinois General Assembly voted to postpone public school choice for Chicago from the 1992/93 to the 1994/95 school year.

Some areas, faced with budget cutbacks, are reducing central offices or reassigning personnel. Montgomery County, Maryland, for example, requires all central office administrators who are certified to spend seven days a year working as substitute teachers. Even the unions are beginning to question the need for layers of central office bureaucrats; in January 1992, the Rochester (New York) Federation of Teachers, an AFT local, purchased a full-page advertisement in the Rochester *Democrat and Chronicle* listing the names, job descriptions, and salaries of 300 administrators they felt should be fired to save money.

The most extensive reform of the central office has happened in Cincinnati. In October 1991, the Cincinnati Business Committee issued a report urging the city's schools to remove central office administrators and simplify that city's school bureaucracy. Superintendent J. Michael Brandt pledged to institute major changes, and was rewarded by Cincinnati voters by a large property tax increase.

In May 1992 Brandt announced that the number of city central office administrators would be cut from 127 to fifty-two; twenty-seven support staff and fifty clerical workers were either transferred or fired, resulting in an expected annual savings of $8 million. All area assistant superintendent positions were eliminated, as well as departments dealing with vocational education, special education, and Chapter 1 programs. The only new person hired was a vice president to deal with business matters, leaving the superintendent free to spend his entire day on educational matters. (The vice president will not be a professional educator.)

Under the plan, teachers and principals would be given more responsibilities. Teachers reported to principals directly,

135

instead of dealing with "instructional supervisors." The city was divided into nine "mini-districts," each made up of a high school, a middle school, and six or seven elementary schools. The head of each mini-district will be a high school principal, who will report directly to the superintendent.

Superintendent Brandt told *Education Week* that these reforms will enable him to spend more time working with teachers and principals and less time dealing with bureaucrats. "I can not have 12 or 14 people directly competing for my time," Brandt said, "on issues not directly impacting on educational issues."[31] While it is too early to judge the Cincinnati reforms, Brandt's plan, if successful, would do more to eliminate central office red tape than any other school district in the country.

Some scholars argue that school restructuring is not sufficient to reform American schools, and that the changes could be better ensured via school choice. "Choice is the logical result of school-based management," RAND researchers Paul T. Hill and Josephine Bonan claim. "If parents are free to choose where they will send their children to school, school staffs have strong incentives to present their goals clearly and offer strong evidence of performance."[32]

Other scholars believe that the central office can be checked in ways that do not involve elaborate restructuring plans. Michigan State education professor Gary Sykes and Harvard's Richard Elmore have several proposals for reform. These include requiring that any level of education bureaucracy proposing a regulation must also include the funds to pay for it. The Department of Education could not mandate state funds; and the states could no longer tell local districts how to spend their dollars. Second, they call for schools to be allowed either to exempt themselves from new regulations or to be able to exempt themselves from regulations in the future if they satisfied the regulation's requirements. Third, all education programs and policies, Sykes and Elmore maintain, should have "sunset" provisions that would automatically terminate them if they were not renewed by Congress or a state legislature. "In the absence of such measures," Sykes and Elmore say, "policymakers will continue to enact requirements as if they were costless and continue to wonder why these requirements have limited and sporadic effects."[33]

Sykes and Elmore's proposals would certainly do some good. Restructuring has also helped schools improve somewhat. But advocates of school restructuring have not yet shown that decentralization, either through school-based management, charter schools, or school councils, is the best way to produce permanent and lasting improvements in American education.

NOTES

1. Cited in David Tyack & Elizabeth Hansot, *Managers of Virtue: Public School Leadership in America, 1820–1980* (New York: Basic Books, 1982), p. 256.
2. Ella Flagg Young, *Isolation in the School* (Chicago: University of Chicago Press, 1901), p. 108.
3. Cited in George S. Counts, *School and Society in Chicago* (New York: Harcourt, Brace, 1928), pp. 77–78.
4. Williard S. Elsbree, *The American Teacher: Evolution of a Profession in a Democracy* (New York: American Book Company, 1939), p. 547.
5. Richard F. Elmore et al., *Restructuring Schools: The Next Generation of Education Reform* (San Francisco: Jossey-Bass, 1990), p. 4.
6. Kenneth A. Sirotnik & Richard W. Clark, "School-Centered Decision Making and Renewal," *Phi Delta Kappan,* May 1988.
7. John E. Chubb & Terry M. Moe, *Politics, Markets, and America's Schools* (Washington, D.C.: Brookings Institution, 1990), p. 201.
8. Betty Malen & Rodney T. Ogawa, "Professional-Patron Influence on Site-Based Governance Councils: A Contending Case Study," *Educational Evaluation and Policy Analysis,* Winter 1988.
9. Betty Malen, Rodney T. Ogawa, & Jennifer Kranz, "What Do We Know About School Based Management? A Case Study of the Literature—A Call for Research." In William H. Clune & John F. Witte, eds., *Choice and Control in American Education* (Philadelphia: Falmer Press, 1990), v. 2, p. 302.
10. Cited in William Snider, "Power Sharing," *Teacher Magazine,* February 1991.
11. Edward B. Fiske, "Miami Schools: Laboratory for Major Changes," *New York Times,* January 10, 1988.
12. *Summative Evaluation Report: School-Based Management/Shared Decision-Making Project, 1987–88 through 1989–90* (Miami: Office of Educational Accountability, Dade County Public Schools, 1991), p. 26.
13. Steven F. Wilson, *Reinventing the Schools: A Radical Plan for Boston* (Boston: Pioneer Institute, 1992), pp. 56–57.
14. Stephanie Gutmann, "Fernandez's Quick Fix," *NY: The City Journal,* Autumn 1991.
15. Ibid.

16. Mary Anne Raywid, "Rethinking School Governance," in Elmore et al., *Restructuring Schools*, p. 158.
17. Paul T. Hill & Josephine Bonan, *Decentralization and Accountability in Public Education* (Santa Monica, CA: RAND, 1991), pp. 11–12.
18. Stuart Sexton, *Opting to Grant-Maintained Schools* (Warlingham, Surrey: Institute for Economic Affairs Education Unit, 1989). The Department for Education was known as the Department of Education and Science until 1992.
19. David Brooks, "Choosing Schools London Style," *NY: The City Journal*, Winter 1991. For a less optimistic view, see Tim Brookes, "A Lesson to Us All," *Atlantic Monthly*, May 1991.
20. "Why Nigel Can't Play," *Wall Street Journal*, July 30, 1991.
21. *Education in England 1990–91: The Annual Report of H M Senior Chief Inspector of the Schools* (London: Department of Education and Science, 1992), p, 21.
22. Ted Kolderie, *Minnesota's New Program of 'Charter Schools,'* (St. Paul, MN: Center for Policy Studies Public Services Redesign Project, 1991); Rhonda Hillbery, "Parental Choice Facing First Major Test," *Los Angeles Times*, August 7, 1991.
23. From a copy of Senate Bill 1448, authored by California State Senator Gary K. Hart.
24. Lynn Olson, "Calif. Is Second State to Allow Charter Schools," *Education Week*, September 20, 1992. Henry Chu, "District Board OKs Pacoima School's Bid for Autonomy," *Los Angeles Times*, May 7, 1993. Louann Bierlein & Lori Mulholland, *Charter Schools: A Viable Reform Alternative* (Tempe, AZ: Morrison Institute for Public Policy, Arizona State University, 1992), give an interesting comparison of the differences between the Minnesota and California charter school bills. K. L. Billingsley, "California's Charter Schools: Empowering Parents, Students, and Teachers" (San Francisco, CA: Pacific Research Institute for Public Policy, April 1993) provides a comprehensive account of California Charter Schools. The Pacific Research Institute's California Project for Educational Innovation will provide information for people interested in creating charter schools.
25. G. Alfred Hess, Jr., *School Restructuring, Chicago Style* (Newbury Park, CA: Corwin Press, 1991), p. xi.
26. Stephen K. Clements & Chester E. Finn, Jr., "Chicago School Reform: A First Year Retrospective and Political Analysis," *Network News and Views*, August 1990.

27. William Ayers, "*Peristroika* in Chicago's Schools," *Educational Leadership*, May 1991.
28. Cited in Robert Guskind, "Rethinking Reform," *National Journal*, May 25, 1991.
29. "Chicago Schools: Must Do Worse," *The Economist*, January 19, 1991.
30. Ellen M. Dran, *The 1990 Illinois Policy Survey* (DeKalb, IL: Center for Governmental Studies, Northern Illinois University, 1990), pp. 10–11.
31. Daniel Gursky, "Cincinnati Cuts More Than Half of Central Office," *Education Week*, June 3, 1992.
32. Hill & Bonan, op. cit., p. 61.
33. Gary Sykes & Richard F. Elmore, "Making Schools Manageable: Policy and Administration for Tomorrow's Schools," in Jane Hannaway & Robert Crowson, eds., *The Politics of Reforming School Administration: The 1988 Yearbook of the Politics of Education Association* (Philadelphia: Falmer Press, 1989), p. 89.

7

SCHOOL CHOICE

"He may not, as unvalu'd persons do
Care for himself, for on his choice depends
The safety and health of the whole state."
William Shakespeare, *Hamlet*

"To compel a man to furnish contributions of money
for the propagation of opinions which he disbelieves and
abhors, is sinful and tyrannical; even forcing him to support
this or that teacher of his own religious persuasion, is
depriving him of the comfortable liberty of giving his con-
tributions to the particular pastor whose morals he would
make his pattern."[1]
Thomas Jefferson, "Bill for the Establishment
of Religious Freedom" (1786)

Should parents be able to use the dollars they pay in taxes to pay for tuition in a private or public school? This question is the most intensely debated issue in American education today. School choice in America has always existed for those able to afford both property taxes and private school tuition. And those parents who could move to the better suburbs have had superior public schools available for their children. But except in Milwaukee, parents unable to flee the city or to purchase tuition have had no say over which schools their children attend. School choice, either among public schools or by using a voucher to pay for tuition in a private school, is increasingly popular with the

American people. In 1971, 43 percent of Americans surveyed by a Gallup poll favored vouchers, and 46 percent were opposed; twenty years later, 50 percent of Americans supported vouchers and only 39 percent were opposed. Support for vouchers is even higher in some states. In 1991, for example, a Reason Foundation poll of California voters reported support for vouchers by a 61 to 28 margin, while the Louisiana Association of Business and Industry found that 59 percent of voters surveyed approved of vouchers.

Polls have consistently shown that support for vouchers or private school choice is highest among people with low incomes and among blacks. A September 1991 survey by the University of Wisconsin (Milwaukee) and the *Milwaukee Community Journal* reported that 76 percent of inner-city blacks supported the state's program of providing up to $2,500 for low-income students to attend private schools. In Detroit, the Wayne State University Center for Urban Governance, in an April 1991 poll, found 53 percent of blacks surveyed favoring a tuition tax credit. Nationally, a May 1991 NBC News/*Wall Street Journal* poll reported 59 percent of blacks surveyed favoring vouchers. As for the poor: Americans with incomes below $15,000 supported vouchers by a 51 to 31 margin nationally in the 1990 Gallup/Phi Delta Kappa poll.[2]

Despite rising public support, private school choice has, as yet, not been implemented outside of Milwaukee. Why has choice been resisted so strenuously by education leaders? To find the answer, one must study how the notion of school choice has changed throughout history. For the story of school choice, at heart, concerns two of the most combustible topics in American politics: race and religion.

In *The Wealth of Nations* (1776), economist Adam Smith argued that public schools should exist, but to provide competition, the salaries of schoolmasters should be partially paid for by tuition to ensure that they were indeed educating students. If a schoolmaster "was wholly, or even principally paid" by the public, Smith taught, "he would soon learn to neglect his business."[3] A generation later, Anglo-American journalist Thomas Paine came very close to inventing the idea of the education

142

voucher. In the second part of *Rights of Man* (1793), Paine proposed that England abolish the "poor rates," a property tax used to assist the unfortunate, and instead give all low-income parents a grant of four pounds annually to send their children to whatever school they pleased. Local ministers, under Paine's proposal, would regularly certify to the state that the grant was being used for education. "By adopting this method," Paine wrote, "the poverty of the parents will be relieved, but ignorance will be banished from the rising generation, and the number of poor will hereafter became less, because their abilities, by the aid of education, will be greater."[4]

Over a half-century later, English philosopher John Stuart Mill, in *On Liberty* (1859), contended that the first principle of British education should be that private and public schools compete for students. Mill was more in favor of government aid to education than either Smith or Paine; he believed, for example, in compulsory education and mandatory national examinations. But he also believed that private schools should be freely established and that the government should pay the tuition charges of all students who qualified for admission. "An education established and controlled by the State," Mill wrote, "should only exist, if it exist at all, as one among many competing experiments."[5] (Mill, like many brilliant Victorians, was educated at home.)

Despite the opinions of these eminent thinkers, private schools in both Britain and America were steadily nationalized throughout the nineteenth century. In England, for example, between 1870 and 1886, 1,124 schools, educating 15 percent of British school children, were taken over by the government. (Church of England schools accounted for 792 of these nationalizations.)

One major exception to this trend was in Vermont. As in most states, Vermont's best high schools were, at first, private academies; then, from 1841 onwards, public high schools began to be established. But in 1869 the city of St. Johnsbury discovered that its children could be educated privately for far less money than it would take to establish a public school. So in that year, the state legislature passed a law that allowed townships that did

143

not have public high schools to pay the tuition costs for students to attend private schools. While this process, known as "tuitioning," has occasionally been modified, particularly by a 1961 Vermont Supreme Court decision banning state funds going to parochial schools, the 1869 law remains in force.

As a result, in ninety-five of Vermont's 246 townships, students have had their expenses paid at private schools. In the 1990/91 school year, for example, 18 percent of Vermont high school students (about 6,000 students) were "tuitioned." Most went to public high schools, but a substantial number went to private schools, including the Phillips Academy, Phillips Exeter, the Deerfield Academy, and Miss Porter's School. Tuitioning largely pays the expenses of some local private academies, such as St. Johnsbury Academy (founded 1842), Lyndon Institute (founded 1847), and Thetford Academy (founded 1815). Without tuitioning, these local institutions would almost certainly either have foundered or have been transformed into public high schools.[6]

Most states, however, did not follow Vermont's example. Private schools were steadily nationalized in the nineteenth century, and politicians frequently attempted to pass laws banning them entirely. One lasting result of these times was the "Blaine Amendment."

In 1875, Speaker of the House James G. Blaine introduced a constitutional amendment stating that no tax dollars used for public schools "shall ever be under the control of any religious sect." The amendment was enthusiastically backed by many leading Republicans, including President Ulysses S. Grant and future president Rutherford B. Hayes, as a tool with which to recoup congressional seats lost to the Democrats in the 1874 mid-term elections. The Blaine Amendment, observes historian Sister Marie Carolyn Klinkhammer, "could be used to attack Catholics, the Irish, southern illiterates, proponents of states' rights, all immigrants from Catholic countries, and anyone else who would make a popular target."[7]

While the Blaine Amendment was swiftly rejected by the House, over two-thirds of the states adopted it as part of their state constitutions; according to the Education Commission of the States, thirty-seven states and Puerto Rico barred state governments from subsidizing private schools. Article VI, Section 2, of the Ohio Constitution, for example, states that "no religious or other sect, or sects, shall ever have any exclusive right to, or control of, any part of the school funds of the state." These state Blaine Amendments still provide a potent barrier against private school choice; Heartland Institute education experts Joseph Bast and Robert Wittman note that one reason parochial schools do not participate in Milwaukee's voucher program is to avoid a court challenge under the state's Blaine Amendment.[8]

As noted in an earlier chapter, it was not until 1925 that the U.S. Supreme Court, in *Pierce v. Society of Sisters*, ruled that private schools were constitutional. But the Pierce decision had two parts. The Court declared that private schools could exist—but that they were subject to government regulation. "No question is raised," said the Court, "concerning the power of the state to reasonably regulate all schools, to inspect, supervise, and examine them, their teachers, and pupils, to require that all children of proper age attend some school, that teachers should be of good moral character and patriotic disposition, that certain studies plainly essential to good citizenship must be taught, and that nothing be taught which is manifestly inimical to the public welfare."[9]

Having determined that private schools had a constitutional right to exist, the Supreme Court then set out to determine what sort of regulations were justified. At first, the Court sought to limit the power of government to control a private school. In *Meyer v. Nebraska* (1923), the Court struck down a law that prohibited teaching foreign language classes (in this case, German) in private schools. Four years later, in *Farrington v. Tokushige* (1927), the Supreme Court ruled that the federal government, as administrator of the Hawaii Territory, had no right to determine either the qualifications of teachers or which textbooks would be used in private schools. Such regulations, declared Justice James McReynolds, would "deprive parents of fair opportunity to procure for their children instruction which they think important."[10] But it was not until thirty years later that the

145

Supreme Court began to shape and determine the nature of the debate over school choice.

When the Supreme Court, in the *Brown* decisions of 1954 and 1955, declared segregated schools unconstitutional, it did not specify how school systems were to be integrated. Eight southern states attempted to satisfy the *Brown* mandate by creating what were known as "free choice" or "schools of choice." Under this scheme, states gave money to parents for tuition in private schools, but usually restricted the tuition grant to segregated schools. Louisiana, for example, gave parents an annual subsidy of $250 to attend a private or public school, but barred integrated schools from receiving many state subsidies, including free textbooks. In some rural areas (most notoriously Prince Edward County, Virginia) the government closed the public school, leaving only private "segregation academies" that refused to admit blacks.

By 1965, only 2 percent of black children in the South were attending integrated schools. The courts then acted to restrict "free choice" plans because they allowed schools to remain segregated. In 1967, the Fifth Circuit Court, while not declaring "free choice" plans unconstitutional, ordered six southern states to integrate their schools, stating that "the only school desegregation plan that meets constitutional standards is one that works."[11]

In the same year, a district court, in *Poindexter v. Louisiana Financial Assistance Commission* (1967), was the first to strike down a state free choice plan, declaring that Louisiana's system of providing "tuition grants" to attend private schools was designed to promote segregation "as certainly as '12' is the next number of a series starting 2, 4, 6, 8, 10."[12] One year later, the Supreme Court, in *Green v. New Kent County* (1968), finally declared "free choice" plans unconstitutional.

Congressional attempts to overturn the *Green* decision were vigorous but futile. On at least three occasions Rep. Jamie Whitten (D–Mississippi) attached an amendment to the Department of Health, Education, and Welfare appropriations bill that would have voided *Green* and allowed for the re-establishment of "free choice" plans. In 1970 the amendment, aided by the endorsement

146

of Nixon administration Attorney General John Mitchell, passed both the House and Senate but ultimately died when President Nixon vetoed the HEW appropriations bill. Nixon's veto meant the end of the "free choice" debate. The war over school choice had shifted to a new battleground—the voucher.

The voucher is one of the few innovations in education whose founding can be definitively traced. The idea that the government should issue a check that parents could use to pay for tuition in a private or public school was invented by Milton Friedman in a 1955 paper. Until Friedman refined the idea in his popular *Capitalism and Freedom* (1962), support for vouchers among conservatives was scanty; Friedrich Hayek, for example, devotes only one paragraph of a chapter on educational reform to vouchers in *The Constitution of Liberty* (1960) . Friedman's idea swiftly proved popular among Catholics. In the first book ever written about school choice, *Freedom of Choice in Education* (1958; revised, 1963), Virgil C. Blum, a Jesuit who taught political science at Marquette University, invented the argument that "parental freedom of choice would establish a buyers' market in the market place of education; every type of school would be forced to offer the best education possible."[13] (In 1957, Blum helped to found Citizens for Educational Freedom, which has remained a leading advocate of school choice ever since.)

By the late 1960s, vouchers had gained some acceptance among educational researchers. In *110 Livingston Street* (1968), for example, David Rogers, after analyzing the failures of New York City's school bureaucracy for several hundred pages, suggested that vouchers were an interesting idea that the city might try to free itself from red tape and stagnation. But it took the efforts of liberal scholars convinced of the need for school choice to make educational vouchers a national issue.

No liberal was more persuasive in the 1960s voucher debate than Christopher Jencks, a Harvard sociologist who had previously been an editor at *The New Republic*. From 1966 onwards, Jencks wrote dozens of pieces in support of vouchers for any publication that would have him (ranging from *The Public Interest* to *The Saturday Evening Post*). His arguments were heard by the Office of Economic Opportunity (OEO), a now defunct federal poverty-fighting organization interested in ways of decentralizing government entitlement programs. In 1969 the OEO gave Jencks and his colleagues $445,000 to write a report describing the ways a voucher program would work. Persuaded by the report, the OEO proposed spending $14 million to subsidize a full-scale test of vouchers in several cities.

The proposals of Jencks and his colleagues were similar to those made by Brookings Institution scholars John Chubb and Terry Moe twenty years later. Jencks did not advocate unrestricted choice; in fact, his "regulated compensatory voucher" would have created a new bureaucracy in Washington, the Education Voucher Agency, to oversee the program and to provide objective reports on the state of schools for parents. Under his plan, low-income parents would have received more money than the better-off, in order that their children might have an advantage in the school marketplace.

Jencks's scheme, despite these restrictions, faced a barrage of criticism. Most national education organizations lobbied intensely against a voucher experiment funded from Washington; the most prominent groups lobbying against vouchers in 1971 were the National Education Association, the American Federation of Teachers, the American Association of School Administrators, the American Jewish Congress, and the Unitarian Universalists. But the low-income parents vouchers were meant to aid were unimpressed with the idea, David K. Cohen and Eleanor Farrar recalled in an article in *The Public Interest,* seeing the scheme as yet another attempt by white professors to tell poor people how to run their lives. "Local civil-rights advocates," Cohen and Farrar wrote, "given their experience with 'freedom of choice' and their knowledge that vouchers were sponsored by the same Nixon administration that opposed busing and favored neighborhood schools, were either hostile or skeptical" to the Jencks plan. Indeed, in Seattle and Rochester, New York, local civil-rights groups lobbied intensely against being included in the voucher test, "which they regarded as either a racist trick or sabotage" that would lead to resegregation.[14]

Support for vouchers, however, did exist. A 1970 Gallup poll reported that 43 percent of Americans favored education vouchers and 46 percent opposed them; one year later, Gallup found 38 percent of Americans supporting the voucher and 44 percent rejecting it. In May 1971, *Phi Delta Kappan*, the journal of the leading national society of education researchers, published a survey of its members that found that 45 percent of the teachers and 29 percent of the administrators who responded favored vouchers. (When asked if parochial schools should receive some tax support, 42 percent of teachers and 35 percent of administrators thought they should.)[15]

Thus while the OEO could find isolated administrators willing to try vouchers (the Superintendent of the schools of East Hartford, Connecticut; the Chairman of the New Hampshire Board of Education) their efforts were blocked by the strenuous lobbying of teacher unions, other education organizations, and some civil rights groups. The only city willing to try vouchers was Alum Rock, California, a poor suburb of San Jose. The OEO test proved little, since the voucher scheme was restricted to public schools, excluded high schools, and did not provide any penalties (such as dismissing and transferring teachers) for unpopular schools. The only lasting lesson of the Jencks exercise was unexpected: School choice would not be implemented from Washington.

That lesson was reinforced by the failures of choice advocates to persuade Congress to provide relief for parents who chose to send their children to private schools. Tuition tax credit bills had been introduced in Congress for decades; as early as 1957, Melvin Laird, then a Republican congressman from Wisconsin, introduced a measure that would have provided a 30 percent tax credit for parents who sent their children to private schools. Tuition tax credit bills passed the Senate five times between 1969 and 1978; in 1978, both the House and Senate approved a tuition tax credit, but the bill failed when the two branches could not agree on whether the credit should apply to all private schools or be limited to colleges and universities.

Attempts by activists to win state funds for private schools by initiatives and referenda also proved fruitless. Between 1966 and 1990, voters turned down 14 referenda that would have provided tax credits or direct subsidies for private schools. The most important of these was a 1981 defeat of a tuition tax credit initiative in the District of Columbia; despite intensive lobbying by such national organizations as the National Taxpayers Union, the initiative was defeated by an 81 to 19 margin.[16]

In the 1980s, despite nominal support from the Reagan administration, supporters of school choice were even less successful than during the previous decade. In 1982 and 1983, tuition tax credit bills died before they were considered by either the House or Senate. Efforts in 1985/86 to turn Chapter 1, the federal education program aiding low-income students, into a voucher also failed. The Bush administration, a more forceful supporter of school choice, also failed to persuade Congress of the merits of the idea; in January 1992, the Senate, by a 57 to 36 margin, defeated a bill that would have provided $30 million in federal funds for vouchers for low-income parents.

All three branches of government, however, have had a say in the school choice debate. In the 1970s and 1980s, the Supreme Court, in a series of convoluted decisions, ensured that school choice, when implemented, would be far more complex than might otherwise have been the case. The Supreme Court's interest in school choice came about through a series of decisions that defined the limits of government aid to parochial schools. When the Court, in the *Meyer*, *Pierce*, and *Farrington* decisions of the 1920s, determined that parochial schools could exist, the rationale for the decision came from the Fifth and Fourteenth Amendments. But when the Court, in *Engel v. Vitale* (1962), outlawed prayer in public schools, it raised the following question. The First Amendment, in a section known as the Establishment Clause, states that "Congress shall make no law respecting an establishment of religion, of prohibiting the free exercise thereof." Does government funding of a church-affiliated school unconstitutionally "establish" or endorse the views of a particular church?

Until *Engel*, the Court relied on *Everson v. Board of Education*, a 1947 decision, for the answer. In *Everson*, the Court, by a 5 to 4 margin, ruled that the state could supply bus transportation for parochial school students, since buses were a subsidy to which all taxpayers were entitled. Government funding of parochial schools was constitutional, the Court ruled, provided that government was neutral towards religion, neither approving nor condemning any expression of faith.

The Court's decisions about church and school in the 1950s were narrow ones. In *McCollum v. Board of Education* (1948), the Court barred private religious teachers from conducting classes during normal public school hours. In *Zorach v. Clawson* (1952), the Court ruled that public school students could be excused during the school day to take classes at churches and synagogues.

Everson, McCollum, and *Zorach,* however, allowed a substantial amount of religion into the public schools. A survey conducted by the University of Chicago in 1956 reported that twelve states and the District of Columbia required daily Bible reading, twenty-five states and New York City permitted Bible readings, while only eleven states prohibited reading the Bible in the classroom (Bible reading was prohibited everywhere in New York except for New York City). A typical ordinance of the era was that of Los Angeles: "It is important that pupils be familiar with such basic Bible passages as the Golden Rule, the Ten Commandments, the Twenty-Third Psalm, and the Beatitudes," said a 1954 Los Angeles manual on teaching morality in the classroom.[17] Moreover, as late as 1957, a national survey reported that two-thirds of the schools in the East and three-quarters of the schools in the South had daily Bible readings.

In 1961, Macalester College education professor Richard Dierenfeld conducted a national survey about the use of religion in the classroom. He found that the Bible was taught in 41.7 percent of America's public school classrooms, with Bible reading taught in 67.6 percent of East Coast schools and 76.8 percent of schools in the South. A third of America's schools held a daily devotion in homerooms before the start of the school day. And 22 percent of the schools surveyed (and 70 percent of southern schools) had regularly scheduled nondenominational religious services.[18] *Engel* not only ended this practice, but it reopened the question of the constitutionality of "parochiaid."

In 1971, the Court finally decided the issue in *Lemon v. Kurtzman* by establishing a three-pronged test that is still law. In

Lemon, the Court declared unconstitutional two state laws: a Rhode Island statute that provided 15 percent of the salaries for teachers of secular subjects in parochial schools, and a Pennsylvania measure that gave some state subsidies to parochial schools for instructional materials and textbooks. Both laws, said the Court, excessively entangled state and church; the Rhode Island measure, in the Court's view, was illegal assistance to the Catholic Church, since the first 250 teachers who applied for salary supplements were all Catholic.

Chief Justice Warren Burger, writing the majority decision, stated that the following three conditions for aid must be met before a parochial school received tax dollars. "First, the statute must have a secular legislative purpose; second, its principal or primary effect must be one that neither advances nor inhibits religion . . . finally, the statute must not foster an excessive government entanglement with religion."[19] But the "wall of separation" between church and state, Chief Justice Burger added, was no wall at all but, "far from being a 'wall,' is a blurred, indistinct, and variable barrier depending on all the circumstances of a particular relationship."[20]

In trying to define this hazy boundary, the Court produced decisions that, by micromanaging the limits of government aid to parochial schools, used the *Lemon* rule to produce judgments best described by Supreme Court Justice Antonin Scalia in 1978, when he was a professor of law at the University of Chicago. "It is impossible," Scalia told the Senate Finance Committee, "within the time allotted, to describe with any completeness the utter confusion of Supreme Court pronouncements in the church-state area."[21] As Sen. Daniel Patrick Moynihan (D–New York) observed, by the early 1980s, students cramming for the District of Columbia bar examination used the following mnemonic to understand the Court's rulings on parochial school aid: government subsidies for items beginning with a "t" (textbooks, transportation, tunafish sandwiches for school lunches) were constitutional; everything else was unconstitutional.

Some examples:

> ⯈ It is constitutional for the state to loan textbooks to parochial schools (*Board of Education v. Allen,* 1968) but uncon-

stitutional for the state to loàn maps, nonreligious periodicals, and laboratory equipment (*Meek v. Pittenger,* 1975).

▶ It is unconstitutional for parochial schools to use government funds to prepare student achievement tests (*Levitt v. Committee for Public Education,* 1973), but constitutional for the state to prepare and provide the same test for parochial schools, even if parochial school teachers do the grading (*Committee for Public Education v. Regan,* 1980).

▶ It is unconstitutional (*Aguilar v. Felton,* 1985) for parochial schools to use federal Chapter 1 funds to supplement the curriculum with remedial math and remedial reading courses, even if the state provided inspectors regularly checked the courses to ensure that moonlighting public school teachers did not teach religion during the after-school study period. But it is constitutional for the same teacher to teach the same course at a neutral site outside the parochial school, such as a diet center. (An analysis by the Congressional Research Service concluded that the Court did not rule on the constitutionality of federally funded courses being transmitted to a parochial school by television, telephone, or radio.)[22]

Such micromanaging is also seen in the three Court decisions that are directly pertinent to the school choice issue. In *Committee for Public Education v. Nyquist* (1973), the Court, in a decision written by Justice Lewis Powell, ruled that a New York state program of tuition tax credits for parochial schools was unconstitutional, since the state provided a grant equalling up to 50 percent of tuition (up to $250) for parents with an annual income of less than $5,000. But in a footnote, Justice Powell suggested that aid to private schools might pass the *Lemon* test if all students, in private or public schools, were entitled to the aid.

Ten years later, Justice Powell's footnote became case law in *Mueller v. Allen* (1983), in which the Court, by a 5 to 4 margin, declared Minnesota's tuition tax deduction constitutional. (Justice Powell cast the deciding vote in *Allen.*) Unlike the New York decision voided in *Nyquist*, the Minnesota program allowed all parents to deduct funds spent on transportation and educational expenses from their state taxes; parents whose incomes were too low to receive the deduction were not entitled to direct state aid. While the Supreme Court has never directly ruled on the constitutionality of vouchers, in 1986 the Court, in *Witters v. Washington Department of Services for the Blind*, unanimously held that a blind Washington student could use a subsidy the state provided to pay for tuition in a Christian college, even though the student planned to become a pastor or a missionary. Though the word "voucher" was not used in *Witters*, the state subsidy approved by the Court closely resembled a voucher plan.

Some legal experts contend that *Witters* is a precedent the Supreme Court will use to declare school vouchers constitutional. But John E. McKeever argues in the *Villanova Law Review* that the Court may well use the *Lemon* test to come up with a different result: declaring vouchers constitutional in states where church-affiliated schools are a minority of private schools (such as in Maine), but ruling that vouchers are unconstitutional in states where parochial schools are a majority of all private schools (such as in Pennsylvania).[23]

The Court's recent decisions in the area of church and state—*Lee v. Weisman* (1992), *Lamb's Chapel v. Center Moriches Union Free School District* (1993), and *Zobrest v. Catalina Foothills School District* (1993)—have done little to change the Court's views, since, in all three decisions, the Court upheld the *Lemon* test. But Justice Scalia, in his concurring opinion in *Lamb's Chapel*, observed that at some point a majority of the current Supreme Court justices have stated their opposition to the *Lemon* rule, and at some point these anti-*Lemon* judges will all agree in one decision. "Like some ghoul in a late-night horror movie that repeatedly sits up in its grave and shuffles around after repeatedly being killed and buried," Justice Scalia warned, "*Lemon* stalks our Establishment Clause jurisprudence once again. No fewer than five of the currently sitting justices have, in their own opinions, personally driven pencils through the creature's heart (the author of today's opinion repeatedly)."[24]

The Supreme Court, as it turned out, would not have to rule

on another form of choice that became popular in the 1970s and 1980s—choice limited to public schools.

The first person to anticipate public school choice was Milton Friedman. In the 1955 essay that introduced the school voucher, Friedman predicted that some form of public choice might well happen. "Perhaps a somewhat greater degree of freedom to choose schools could be made available in a governmentally administered system" Friedman wrote, "but it is hard to see how it could be carried very far in view of the obligation of every child with a place" in the schools.[25]

But the public school choice movement really began in the late 1960s. In that turbulent time, some school systems, striving to please students prone to strikes and other forms of dissent, created a series of alternative schools. In Berkeley, California, for example, students could choose between a traditional school (known as "Model A High"), a school for blacks, and "Genesis High," an experimental institution where students were divided into "tribes" instead of classes. (The local PTA was abolished and replaced by an "Inter-Tribal Council.")

Most of these alternative schools, like many other fads of the 1960s, faded away, as school superintendents lost a taste for experimentation and federal grantmakers decided that their funds could not be used to subsidize public schools that arbitrarily restricted enrollment by race or gender. But the notion that public high schools did not have to be the same had struck many educational researchers as viable. Thus the alternative school idea gradually evolved into public school choice.

The catalyst here was Mario D. Fantini, one of the architects of the failed New York City school decentralization effort of the late 1960s. Living in northeastern New Jersey in one of New York's bedroom suburbs, Fantini tried to enroll his son in a school in another town, only to be told by that town's school superintendent that such a transfer "would interrupt our whole administrative organization."[26] Unable to afford either private school tuition or a new house, Fantini wondered why parents couldn't choose among public schools. Why couldn't parents, Fantini thought, be free to choose a school in another city if that school offered programs from which their children could benefit.

So in 1973 Fantini published *Public Schools of Choice,* the first book on the subject. In it, Fantini argued that choosing between public schools could provide the benefits of school choice without the controversy and divisiveness of the voucher wars. "Using education vouchers," Fantini wrote, "to make options outside the public school system—the external voucher plan—is far less important, far less desirable, than creating options within the system and making these available, by choice, to parents, students, and teachers."[27]

Although Fantini's ideas would not be implemented for fifteen years, some moves toward public school choice did occur in the 1970s. Some school systems began to diversify their schools, most notably District 4 in New York City's East Harlem area. Starting in 1974, District 4 slowly began to change its schools, so that, by the mid-1980s, students could choose between a wide range of elementary and junior high schools. Test scores improved substantially, and students, teachers, and parents became more satisfied with the education the city provided.[28]

Public school choice was first tried as a way to solve the problems created by school busing. By 1975 it was clear that, in most cases, school busing was doing little good and a great deal of harm. In several cities, "white flight" was taking place, as parents fled to the suburbs rather than have their children spend hours on a school bus. When white parents stayed in place, they fiercely resisted busing plans. In Boston, the northern city where school busing was most divisive, Judge J. Arthur Garrity not only took over operation of the schools but issued over 400 court orders regulating school affairs, including one controlling the amount of toilet paper that schools could purchase.

As the white percentage of urban school students fell, judges began to order schools to spend money on frills to entice students back into a city's public schools. In Kansas City, Missouri, for example, Judge Russell Clark ruled in 1984 that white flight had resulted in segregating the city's school system, even though Kansas City had never had school busing. He ordered the city and the state of Missouri to provide amenities to ensure that the percentage of white students in Kansas City schools rose from 26 percent to 40 percent.

To satisfy the court mandate, Blake Hurst reported in *Reason*, the city and state spent lavishly, spending nearly $1 billion to equip Kansas City schools with swimming pools, greenhouses, racquetball courts, an art gallery, a zoo, and at least one log cabin. One Kansas City school spent $1.3 million on a field house and $150,000 on a weight room.

In the summer of 1991, Judge Clark ordered Missouri to spend $71 million—10 percent of the state's total education budget—to cover overruns in school construction programs. In 1991, Missouri spent $10,000 per student to combat segregation in Kansas City, only spending $1,000 per student in the rest of the state.[29] Admittedly, Kansas City is an extreme case, but it nonetheless illustrates how busing programs, in the name of aiding poor blacks, frequently turn into subsidies for well-to-do whites.

In her book *School Desegregation Outcomes for Children* (1975), Nancy St. John of the University of Massachusetts (Boston) reviewed 120 studies of school desegregation and concluded that the program "must be judged neither a demonstrated success nor a demonstrated failure." School busing did not harm white or black students, but the evidence that busing improved academic achievement was "mixed, intermittent, or nonsignificant."[30]

"The 120 studies of school desegregation represent a tremendous investment of federal and foundation funds and professional endeavor," St. John added, "an investment that in retrospect seems largely wasted."[31] Rather than resorting to elaborate, court-mandated busing schemes, St. John suggested that cities might try school choice, limited to schools in one district, and controlled to ensure that desegregation plans were met. Desegregation might be more successful, St. John said, "if families were allowed some choice (not unlimited choice) between schools of various educational philosophies, of various social and racial clienteles, and at various distances from home."[32]

Such programs, technically known as "intradistrict controlled choice," were instituted in some American cities in the 1970s and 1980s. Controlled-choice programs proved to be most popular in Massachusetts. They were first instituted in Springfield, Massachusetts in 1972; by 1990, such systems were in place in Fall River, Lawrence, Lowell, Worcester, Cambridge, and five other cities. Boston replaced its school busing program with controlled choice in the 1990/91 school year.

Educational experts are divided on the efficacy of controlled choice. Abigail Thernstrom, an education expert who formerly taught at Harvard and Boston College, contends in *School Choice in Massachusetts* (1991) that controlled choice plans are ineffective because parents are frequently unable to make informed choices, and when they do make choices, they make bad ones, choosing a school because of its football team instead of its honors programs.

After studying Massachusetts's choice programs, she concluded that parents could not make intelligent choices for two reasons. First, the school guides given to parents were too vague; every school in Worcester appeared "to be committed to two things: recognizing diversity and using computers."[33] Second, the "market" in schools created by controlled choice does not allow for failure; bad schools rather than being closed, received additional state aid. "Unpopular schools are not being shut down and popular schools are not being replicated to any particular degree."[34]

Steven F. Wilson, co-director of the Pioneer Institute, observes in his recent book *Reinventing the Schools*, that controlled choice plans in Boston are still under court jurisdiction; the head of Boston's controlled choice program, Catherine Ellison, is on the payroll of the Boston Public Schools but is appointed by the court and cannot be fired by the school system. In an interview, Ellison explained to Wilson that she saw her job as allocating assignments of pupils to schools, a job that was "not in the field of education." "For Ellison and her staff," Wilson believes, "controlled choice is a numbers game" designed to implement racial quotas.[35]

Charles Glenn, an education professor at Boston University who spent nearly two decades in the Massachusetts Department of Education creating desegregation plans, has a more optimistic view of controlled choice. Writing in *The Public Interest,* Glenn contends that most parents using controlled-choice programs choose good schools, and those parents who choose bad schools are hardly more immoral than a school system that mandates that children attend a school that might be below average. Public school choice, he believes, is "a powerful way to expand the options available to poor families, and to put pressure on urban schools to become both more effective and more responsive."[36]

Do parents under a school choice plan choose schools badly? Some additional evidence in answer to this question comes from educational researchers studying recent reforms in Minnesota. Minnesota is the first state where students are free to choose among public schools. Although the state has had a strong tradition of promoting educational diversity (a tuition tax deduction has been in place since 1955), public school choice took nearly a decade to develop. First proposed in 1982 by the Citizens League, a statewide reform group, public school choice was not a subject of political debate until 1985, when Democratic Governor Rudy Perpich proposed allowing qualified high school juniors and seniors to attend the college of their choice, and to have their tuition paid by the state. His bill passed, despite mass opposition—both national teacher unions, the state associations of school boards and superintendents, the speaker of the Minnesota House, and the majority leader of the Senate.

Other choice bills swiftly followed. In 1987, students who were performing poorly in school were allowed to transfer freely to a more suitable school. In the 1989/90 school year, choice was introduced to districts with over 1,000 students; in 1990/91, to the entire state.

Minnesota's programs have been widely lauded, but relatively few parents have actually chosen to transfer their children to other schools; in the 1989/90 school year, only 3,218 students, or about 0.5 percent of the children in Minnesota schools, enrolled in other districts. Ross Corson, writing in *The American Prospect,* notes other restrictions on Minnesota school choice: school boards can limit transfers from other districts (particularly if the district is part of a desegregation plan) or opt out of the program entirely if they so choose. School counselors must also interview—and approve—all transfers from other districts. "Open enrollment in Minnesota," Corson contends, "is hardly a free market in education."[37]

Moreover, it was a "market" that many parents found difficult and confusing to follow, as educators tried to cloak the minor differences between their schools in bureaucratic jargon. Bonnie Blodgett, a parent in St. Paul, Minnesota, wrote a piece for *Lear's* magazine in which she described how difficult it was to determine which school would be the best one for her daughter to attend. "The magnet program guide was not terribly enlightening," she wrote. "Every school promised to bring out the particular interests and strength of our child, to build her confidence, character, and social skills. Every school differed in the methods deployed to effect these happy results, but evaluating that difference, whether it was an experimental teaching method or immersion in a particular subject, was difficult. The literature teemed with educationese—developmentally appropriate and child-centered learning methodologies. These illusive bits of jargon darted in and out of our minds like minnows."[38]

Still, until 1990, Minnesota allowed more school choice than any other state in the nation. But in that year, the Wisconsin legislature passed a bill authorizing Milwaukee's public schools to try something that no one else had tried—a voucher program for low-income students.

A similar program had nearly been created twenty years before. In 1968, in the aftermath of Martin Luther King's assassination, the California state legislature appointed a commission to study the schools in low-income areas. The commission concluded that "the sorry state of education in ghetto schools probably results from the monopolistic hold that the public schools have in poor and minority children,"[39] and introduced a bill that would have given low-income parents the right to apply for vouchers, create their own school districts, and pool their vouchers either to create their own schools or hire contractors to run them.

The California Assembly never considered the bill, but a 1968 study conducted by the University of California (Los Angeles) Survey Research Center of parents living in the Watts ghetto in Los Angeles found that 79.3 percent of them favored the bill and 66 percent thought the schools would improve if parents had choice.

What Wisconsin had that California lacked was Polly Williams, a black Democratic state representative with a checkered career, including serving as Jesse Jackson's campaign coordinator in the state during the 1984 and 1988 primaries. Some critics charged that she was a militant; writing in *The New Republic*, Ben Wildavsky observed that Williams had the title of "general of education" in a "Black Panther militia" organized by Michael McGee, a Milwaukee alderman who had written letters to Saddam Hussein advocating "the overthrow of the U.S. government if conditions don't change by 1995."[40]

Williams first proposed, in 1986, carving a separate school district in Milwaukee that would be controlled by blacks. When that idea failed, Williams successfully put together a coalition of Republicans, conservative Democrats, and blacks favoring school choice. In May 1990, the Wisconsin legislature passed a bill that provided vouchers of up to $2,500 annually for up to one percent of the children in Milwaukee public schools. To qualify, parents had to have incomes no higher than 175 percent of the national poverty rate. In a 1990 interview with *Reason*, Williams explained that two of her primary reasons for supporting school choice were her distaste of magnet schools and busing. The Milwaukee school system, Williams told the *Wall Street Journal*'s John Fund, was "busing kids from one black elementary school in this area to 104 different schools. A group of African American parents is going to propose that we modify this busing madness and start building schools kids can walk to again."

"This paternalistic notion that poor people can't make choices is ridiculous," Williams added. "Poor people are some of the best shoppers, most skilled at stretching a dollar, you'll ever see."[41]

Milwaukee's choice experiment has gotten off to a slow start. Foes of the program spent two years trying to kill it in the courts, forcing the test to begin with the understanding that it could be declared unconstitutional at any time. In the 1990/91 school year, only 600 parents applied for 400 positions, even though approximately 60,000 of the 90,000 students in the Milwaukee system had parents with incomes low enough to qualify. By year's end, only 252 students were using vouchers, and only 195 of these returned for a second year in the program. (But other students joined, bringing the number of Milwaukee students using choice in the 1991/92 school year to about 575.)

An evaluation of the Milwaukee plan by the Wisconsin Department of Public Instruction provides some positive evidence for the program. The evaluation, conducted by John F. Witte, a political scientist at the University of Wisconsin (Madison), surveyed parents and teachers and found some evidence for increased parental involvement and teacher satisfaction. Parents whose children were in the choice program, for example, tended to go to parent-teacher association meetings and student evaluations about 5 percent more often than they did when their children went to public schools.

Witte concluded that it was too early to determine whether the Milwaukee parental choice program was a success for several reasons. Nearly all of the students were in elementary and junior high schools, and at that age it was difficult to measure any student's achievement with precision. Until students reach high school, Witte wrote, "grades are rarely given or have little meaning, attendance generally varies little, suspensions are very seldom given at the elementary level, and (as is true of high school) vary from school to school depending on administrative rules and the philosophy of principals."[42]

Given the legal uncertainty of the program and the small number of students enrolled, Witte said that very little could be concluded about the Milwaukee voucher program. But the success of parental choice so far led Witte to contend that Milwaukee's plan should be continued "for at least several more years. Despite some problems and difficulties, engendered both by the uncertainty of the program's future (because of court challenges) and by limited demonstrated educational success to date, it is clear this program continues to offer opportunities otherwise unavailable to some Milwaukee parents."[43]

The Wisconsin Supreme Court's declaration in March 1992

that the Milwaukee voucher program was constitutional may ensure that the experiment will be more successful in the future. The Milwaukee public schools, however, have made some changes to compete with the voucher program. In January 1992, the city's school board authorized the creation of chartered schools beginning in the 1992/93 school year. In June 1992, Milwaukee Superintendent Howard Fuller proposed reducing property taxes and allowing principals control over individual school budgets. And Milwaukee Mayor John O. Norquist, in an article in *Wisconsin Interest*, called for the city's public schools to "ultimately be scrapped" and replaced with "a voucher or choice system. We should give city parents the purchasing power they need to enroll their children in any public or private, non-sectarian school that complies with essential standards."[44]

In April 1992, Norquist told a group of Milwaukee Catholic school leaders that the parochial schools in his city would soon receive public aid as a consequence of the success of school choice. State aid to parochial schools "is more practical in Milwaukee than it is in any place in the United States right now," Norquist said, "because we already won the battle for the non-religious schools. We're ready for the next step."[45]

Thus very little can be said about the success or failure of private school choice in America. But additional evidence about choice can be found in Canadian and English schools. In Canada, education has been a provincial matter. In some provinces, parochial schools, like their American counterparts, are privately funded. In other provinces, as in most European nations, sectarian schools are state funded.

In the late 1970s Donald Erickson, a professor in the Graduate School of Education at the University of California (Los Angeles), decided to compare Catholic schools in various Canadian provinces, contrasting completely tax-funded schools (in Alberta, Saskatchewan, and Ontario) with comparable schools in Manitoba and British Columbia that received no governmental aid.

Erickson found that more Catholics sent their children to state-funded Catholic schools than private ones, since, in many cases, they were required by law to do so. But government funds had "deprivatized" Catholic schools, "attenuating or obliterating numerous characteristics which elsewhere distinguished Catholic schools from public schools."[46] Erickson also discovered that government controlled Catholic schools tended to have weaker connections with the local parish and teachers less committed to Catholic thinking than systems where Catholic schools remained completely private.

In a second study, Erickson analyzed British Columbia schools. In 1978 British Columbia began a program of subsidizing 30 percent of private school costs. Since these subsidies went to the school instead of to the parent or the student, the British Columbia program was not a voucher plan. In this plan, schools tended to use the subsidies to raise teacher salaries rather than cut tuition; and the parents Erickson surveyed were less involved in their schools than before, since they could not see how the government funds benefited them. Moreover, with government funds came government regulation. Mandatory consumer education programs were introduced, and private school students were required to pass the provincial examinations that public school students had to take. Schools altered their courses to spend more time studying for the test; in some cases, schools replaced religious education programs with courses in test-taking.

"More important," Erickson writes, "the principle had been established that government, which had almost totally ignored private schools when they received no public aid, would now regulate them; statutory demands now in the rule books would be given a more onerous interpretation by a less benevolent government."[47]

Britain has always had more varied forms of aid to private schools than America, and there the growth and consolidation of state schools took far longer. The controversies over aid to religious schools, moreover, did not exist, because England, unlike America, had an established church, and all schools, whether state or private, were required to provide some form of religious instruction.

Britain's Education Act of 1944 created three forms of state aid for private schools. "Government-maintained" schools, mostly affiliated with the Church of England, were institutions that received their entire budget from the state but had a few private members of the school's board of governors. "Government-aided" schools were schools, many Catholic, that received 85 percent of their budget from the state, and had independent authority to hire and fire teachers. "Direct grant" schools were tuition-charging private institutions that received 75 percent of their budget from the state as a block grant in return for providing free tuition for one-quarter of the students who met the school's entrance standards.

Many members of the Labour Party and the Trades Union Congress hated private schools; in the 1940s, Labourites attempted to ban private schools entirely. But an overall school shortage and narrow majorities during most Labour administrations ensured that the 1944 Education Act remained unamended until 1975, when the second Harold Wilson administration abolished direct grant schools, telling these schools that they either had to come under state control or become private institutions. Fifty-one of these schools, mostly Catholic, became government aided; the remaining 119 refused subsidies and were privatized.

The Conservative Party had long championed private schools; as late as 1980, three-quarters of the Tory members of Parliament were educated privately. Conservative leader Margaret Thatcher was particularly interested in the schools; from 1971 to 1974, she had been Minister of Education in the administration of Edward Heath. Thus, when the Conservatives returned to power in 1979, one of their first acts was to restore direct grant schools.

The Thatcher administration never attempted to create any sort of universal voucher plan. The leading British voucher advocacy group, the Friends of the Education Voucher Experiment, could not even get their proposals considered by the Department of Education and Science. But Parliament, as part of the Education Act of 1980, created the "assisted-places scheme."

The assisted-places scheme resembles the voucher program in Milwaukee. Parents with low incomes who have children age 11 to 18 can have their children apply for admission in private day schools. (Boarding schools were deliberately excluded.) If these private schools accept a student, the government will pay some or all of the cost of tuition, based on a means-tested sliding scale. For the 1991/92 school year, parents with incomes below 8,714 pounds have the entire cost of tuition paid for by the state; parents with annual incomes above 16,902 pounds must pay one-third of the tuition. The grants to assisted-place students are secret; only the headmaster and the school treasurer know which students receive government subsidies.

In the decade since the assisted-places scheme was introduced, nearly 50,000 students have benefited; in the 1991/92 school year, about 27,000 assisted-place students were enrolled in private schools, at a cost to the British taxpayer of about 7 million pounds annually. Many old and worthy private day schools have accepted assisted-place students, including Westminster School, Winchester College, and Dulwich College, whose alumni include P. G. Wodehouse and Raymond Chandler.

When the assisted-places scheme was first proposed in 1980, the Labour Party's Neil Kinnock (shadow education minister at the time) claimed that the assisted-places scheme would be one of the "greasy poles scaled most easily by the crammed and pampered offspring of the middle class."[48] The most extensive analysis of the assisted-places scheme suggests that Kinnock's fears were overstated.

From 1984 to 1987, University of London sociologists Tony Edwards, John Fitz, and Geoff Whitty talked to teachers, parents, and students to find out how the assisted-places scheme affected education. They found that schools were eager to have assisted-place students—so much so that the number of places available constantly exceeded the supply of qualified students. (In the 1990/91 school year, for example, only 81 percent of the assisted places available to students were filled; over 4,000 places were vacant.) Some schools accepted assisted-place students as part of their tradition of public service; others thought the less well off would provide a useful balance to the snobbery of the children of the nouveau riche. Still other schools thought bright low-income students might help revive moribund organizations. In a school the authors called "Cathedral College," the head teacher explained that assisted-places students were welcomed because "of the old thing of the nobility freshening the blood by marrying pretty shop girls. I think it's the same principle really, introducing fresh blood to the school."[49]

Edwards and his colleagues found that assisted-places children did well on national examinations and that the scheme enabled parents to send their children to schools they would have otherwise never considered. The authors surveyed parents of assisted-places children and found that 62 percent of them chose a private school because of the institution's values; 57 percent because of the likelihood that private school attendance would increase the chances of getting into a university; and only 8 percent because of a family tradition of sending children to private schools.

But the low-income parents Edwards surveyed tended not to be working class. Only 10 percent were employed as manual workers (such as bus drivers, factory workers, and miners). About 50 percent were "service class" employees—teachers, police officers, social workers, middle managers, and so forth. Most of these were relatively well educated but had depressed incomes due to disability, unemployment or underemployment, or divorce; 40 percent of the assisted place scheme families were single-parent households.

There was little evidence, Edwards and his colleagues concluded, that the assisted-places scheme helped the children of the working class climb the social ladder. Their research suggested that assisted-place children were "not clearly from socially or culturally disadvantaged backgrounds, despite the relatively low incomes of their parents."[50]

The likelihood that the assisted-places scheme will be expanded into a full-scale voucher is small. The Labour Party has vowed to eliminate the program should it return to power. The Conservatives are divided into two camps; Tories who agree with Prime Minister John Major that government efficiency is a more worthy goal than privatization, and Thatcherite politicians who believe that government funds should not interfere with a free market.

The stories of school choice in Britain and Canada thus

provide two valuable lessons for American school reformers. First, advocates of private school choice need to ensure that government regulations not follow the government dollar to school. Certainly the federal entitlement programs that are voucher-like (food stamps, housing subsidies) are as riddled with waste, fraud, and red tape as entitlements that do not use voucher mechanisms. Can advocates of school choice say with confidence that a private school that accepts vouchers will not be under the complete control of state education agencies and local school boards?

Second, care must be taken to ensure that low-income parents receive as much information about schools as possible in as many different ways as possible. Critics of school choice usually charge that a voucher program will create "creaming"—private schools will get the brightest students and public schools will be stuck with the leftovers. School choice, author Jonathan Kozol told the *Washington Post*, creates "a system of triage that will enable the most fortunate to opt out and leave large numbers of the poorest and least sophisticated people in schools nobody would willingly choose."[51]

The evidence from Great Britain suggests that Kozol's vision is somewhat simplified. Private schools did manage to reach low-income parents, but they found that traditional methods of communication (newspapers, announcements) did not reach the lower classes. Some schools found that fliers at gas stations and take-out restaurants were effective; others found radio advertisements fruitful. But the most effective advertisement was what one head teacher called "the parental bush telegraph"—parents telling their friends about good schools.

Thus it may well be that, over time, reliable information about schools will reach parents in a variety of ways. Certainly one can foresee entrepreneurs creating guides to high schools that resemble existing guides to colleges and universities. It is also clear that poor people's lack of income does not make them, as a class, foes of education and culture. One of the major themes of American history and literature, after all, is that of immigrants—from Ireland, Poland, Africa, Asia, and elsewhere—who teach their children to study, work hard, and climb the social ladder. Certainly if poor people were as invincibly ignorant as Kozol suggests, neither Ronald Reagan nor Jesse Jackson would have succeeded.

But it is equally clear that some advocates of school choice have overstated their case. Both public and private school choice have flaws in their plans that must be corrected if they are to succeed. Advocates of public school choice must provide evidence that any program that allows choice among public schools will be permanent and lasting. As an internal reform in school systems, public school choice plans can easily be overturned. In Des Moines, Iowa, for example, that city's school board recently barred 121 white students from transferring to suburban schools on the grounds that such transfers would upset the racial balance of Des Moines schools, currently 20 percent black. Because Iowa state educational aid is apportioned by the student, such out-of-the-city transfers are quite costly for Des Moines schools; a study prepared by the Des Moines school system charged that the Iowa public school choice plan cost Des Moines 279 students and $1.2 million in aid in two years, and might cost the city $7.4 million over five years.[52]

Parents are currently suing the Des Moines schools over their failure to allow transfers out of the city. Should these parents' requests be denied, it is likely that other cities, particularly older ones with large minority enrollments, might also try to end or water down public school choice programs. Should that happen, public school choice will become as ineffectual as school-based management, merit pay, and other failed reforms.

Like other reforms, public school choice cannot succeed if it is imposed from the top down, if it is presented as yet another mandate from the state department of education to local school boards. TEACH Michigan researchers Adam Devore and Robert Wittman report that the success or failure of public school choice in that state largely depends on whether or not a local school system supported the reforms. Wyandotte, Michigan, had already implemented a choice plan when the statewide public school began and used the state's resources to complement its own efforts.

But as early as April 1992, Devore and Wittman report, "it

appeared that the *majority* of districts perceived the schools of choice legislation not as an opportunity for genuine innovation and experimentation, but rather as another burdensome mandate for which the legislature was providing little or no funding."[53]

Some school districts in Michigan complained that the state had not provided enough money to school buses; others loosened their transfer policies but did not make any other changes; still others declared that their space was so limited that they could take few out-of-district students. But the most articulate criticism of the Michigan public school choice plan came from the Alpena schools, which noted in a brochure that there was little difference between that city's public schools. Alpena had ten elementary schools, the brochure noted, each of which "has a different building, a different teaching staff, and serves a different neighborhood. Beyond that, there are no substantive differences. Each runs on basically the same program, teaches the same curriculum, offers the same basic dollars per pupil education. For choice to be real, there has to be a real difference between schools."[54]

If public school choice is to be a successful reform, then public schools must offer sufficient variety for an internal market to be created. In some areas, magnet schools may provide the foundations for such a market; the charter school movement may provide another alternative. But in areas where public school choices are substantially the same, students are as likely to change schools because of quirks in the school boundary lines or out of a desire to play on a winning sports team rather than a losing one. Public school choice may be helpful in changing the schools, but it cannot be a success in a homogenous, monolithic school system.

Advocates of private school choice should take care not to overstate the benefits that this reform might bring to the schools. "Choice is a self-contained reform with its own rationale and justification," John Chubb and Terry Moe write in their influential *Politics, Markets, and America's Schools.* "It has the capacity all by itself to bring about the transformation that, for years, reform-

170

ers have been seeking for years to engineer in myriad other ways."[55]

But school choice will not convince parents that education is worthwhile, tell students to do their homework, teach right and wrong, dissolve all red tape, or even ensure that students are as educated as their parents or grandparents. Certainly school choice will provide some improvements in schools, but these improvements will probably be incremental and take place over time. The available evidence suggests that the benefits school choice will provide American schools are more gradual and less dramatic than either friends or foes of the reform contend will take place.

NOTES

1. Cited in Thomas James & Henry M. Levin, eds., *Public Dollars and Private Schools: The Case of Tuition Tax Credits* (Philadelphia: Temple University Press, 1983), p. 153.
2. These polls are collected in *Public Opinion on Choice in Education* (Washington, D.C.: Center for Choice in Education, U.S. Department of Education, 1992). See also Patrick J. Keleher, Jr., *Out of Touch: Educational Leadership v. Grass-roots Leadership on School Choice* (Chicago: TEACH America, 1992), for other polls on school choice. The Home Box Office poll is mentioned in E. J. Dionne, "In Poll, Blacks Defy Political Stereotyping," *Washington Post,* July 9, 1992.
3. Adam Smith, *An Inquiry into the Nature and Causes of the Wealth of Nations,* ed. R. H. Campbell & A. S. Skinner (Indianapolis: Liberty Classics, 1981), p. 785.
4. Thomas Paine, *Rights of Man,* ed. Henry Collins (Baltimore: Penguin, 1969), p. 263.
5. Cited in George R. LaNoue, ed. *Educational Vouchers: Concepts and Controversies* (New York: Teachers College Press, 1972), p. 4.
6. The best account of "tuitioning" is John McClaughry, *Educational Choice in Vermont* (Concord, VT: Institute for Liberty and Community, 1987).
7. Sister Marie Carolyn Klinkhammer, "The Blaine Amendment of 1875: Private Motives for Political Action," *Catholic Historical Review,* April 1956.
8. Joseph Bast & Robert Wittmann, "Educational Choice Design Barriers," in Joseph Bast & Diane Bast, eds., *Rebuilding America's Schools: Vouchers, Credits, and Privatization* (Chicago: Heartland Institute, 1991), p. 26.
9. James & Levin, op. cit., p. 190.
10. Cited in David W. Kirkpatrick, *Choice in Schooling: A Case for Tuition Vouchers* (Chicago: Loyola University Press, 1990), p. 26.
11. Cited in George R. Metcalf, *From Little Rock to Boston: The History of School Desegregation* (Westport, CN: Greenwood Press, 1983), pp. 10–11.
12. Cited in LaNoue, op. cit., p. 31.

13. Virgil C. Blum, S. J., *Freedom of Choice in Education* (New York: Macmillan, 1958), p. 147.
14. David K. Cohen & Eleanor Farrar, "Power to the Parents?—The Story of Education Vouchers," *The Public Interest,* Summer 1977.
15. "Educational Accountability," *Phi Delta Kappan,* May 1971.
16. A highly partisan analysis of these votes, written by foes of school choice, is provided in Edd Doerr & Albert J. Menendez, *Church Schools and Public Money: The Politics of Parochiaid* (Buffalo, NY: Prometheus Books, 1991). pp. 69–85.
17. Cited in Richard Dierenfeld, *Religion in American Public Schools* (Washington, D.C.: Public Affairs Press, 1962), p. 43.
18. Ibid., p. 66.
19. Cited in John E. McKeever, "'Forbidden Fruit': Governmental Aid to Nonpublic Education and the Primary Effect Test Under the Establishment Clause," *Villanova Law Review,* November 1989.
20. Cited in Michael Barnes, "The *Lemon* Test and the Establishment Clause: A Proposal for Modification," *Golden Gate University Law Review,* Summer 1990.
21. Cited in Daniel Patrick Moynihan, "What Do You Do When the Supreme Court is Wrong," in Nathan Glazer, ed., *The Public Interest on Education* (Cambridge, MA: Abt Books, 1984), p. 125. An excellent analysis of the convoluted constitutional history of parochial school aid is provided in Jesse H. Choper, "The Establishment Clause and Aid to Parochial Schools—An Update," *California Law Review,* January 1987.
22. See *After Aguilar v. Felton: Chapter 1 Services to Nonpublic Schoolchildren* (Washington, D.C.: U.S. House of Representatives, Committee on Education and Labor, 1986).
23. McKeever, op. cit.
24. See "Excerpts from Supreme Court Decision in *Lamb's Chapel Case,*" *Education Week,* June 16, 1993.
25. Milton Friedman, "The Role of Government in Education," in Robert A. Solo, ed., *Economics and the Public Interest* (Rutgers, NJ: Rutgers University Press, 1955), p. 129.
26. Mario Fantini, *Public Schools of Choice* (New York: Simon & Schuster, 1973), p. 17.
27. Ibid., p. 20.
28. David L. Kirp, "What School Choice Really Means," *The Atlantic Monthly,* November 1992. A more pessimistic assessment is provided by Billy Tashman in "Hyping District 4," *The New*

Republic, December 7, 1992. The most comprehensive account of the District 4 story is Seymour Fliegel with James MacGuire, *Miracle in East Harlem: The Fight for Choice in Public Education* (New York: Times Books, 1993).

29. Blake Hurst, "Everything's Up to Date," *Reason,* March 1992.
30. Nancy St. John, *School Desegregation Outcomes for Children* (New York: John Wiley, 1975), p. 119.
31. Ibid., p. 122. Since 1975, the evidence that desegregation has improved school achievement is slight, since there is little difference in the rises in test scores of black children in segregated and desegregated schools. See David J. Armor, "Why Is Black Educational Achievement Rising?", *The Public Interest,* Summer 1992.
32. Ibid., p. 132.
33. Abigail Thernstrom, *School Choice in Massachusetts* (Boston: Pioneer Institute, 1991), p. 42.
34. Ibid., p. 45.
35. Steven F. Wilson, *Reinventing the Schools: A Radical Plan for Boston* (Boston: Pioneer Institute, 1992), p. 11.
36. Charles Glenn, "Controlled Choice in Massachusetts Public Schools," *The Public Interest,* Spring 1991.
37. Ross Corson, "Choice Ironies: Open Enrollment in Minnesota," *The American Prospect,* Fall 1990.
38. Bonnie Blodgett, "The Private Hell of Public Education," *Lear's,* April 1992.
39. Cited in Robert Singleton, "California: The Self-Determination in Education Act, 1968" in *Parents, Teachers, and Children: Prospects for Choice in American Education* (San Francisco: Institute for Contemporary Studies, 1977), p. 80.
40. Ben Wildavsky, "Hero of Choice," *The New Republic,* October 23, 1990.
41. John Fund, "Champion of Choice: An Interview with Polly Williams," *Reason,* October 1990.
42. John F. Witte, *First Year Report Milwaukee Parental Choice Program* (Madison, WI: Department of Public Instruction, 1991), p. 8.
43. Ibid, p. 3.
44. John O. Norquist, "The Future of Our Cities," *Wisconsin Interest,* Winter/Spring 1992. Mayor Norquist expands on these views in an article in the July 1993 *Reader's Digest.*
45. Marie Rohde, "Norquist Says Parochial Schools Will Soon Get Public Money," *Milwaukee Journal,* April 28, 1992.

46. Donald Erickson, "Choice and Private Schools: Dynamics of Supply and Demand," in Daniel C. Levy, ed., *Private Education: Studies in Choice and Public Policy* (New York: Oxford University Press, 1986), p. 97.
47. Ibid., p. 101.
48. Cited in Tony Edwards, John Fitz, & Geoff Whitty, *The State and Private Education: An Evaluation of the Assisted Places Scheme* (London: Falmer Press, 1989), p. 70.
49. Ibid., p. 102.
50. Ibid., p. 161.
51. Cited in Linda Chion-Kenney, "The Choice Debate," *Washington Post*, February 10, 1992.
52. Edward Walsh, "Des Moines Cities 'White Flight' in Curbing School Choice," *Washington Post*, December 11, 1992.
53. Adam Devore & Robert Wittman, *Michigan's Experiment with Public School Choice: A First Year Assessment* (Midland, MI: Mackinac Center, 1993), p. 3.
54. Ibid., pp. 7–8.
55. John Chubb & Terry Moe, *Politics, Markets, and America's Schools* (Washington, D.C.: Brookings Institution, 1990), p. 217.

FOR
FURTHER
READING

A great deal has been written about American education. Much of it is of interest, but to find the books worth reading requires a good deal of time and patience. To assist the reader, I have prepared the following annotated bibliography. Most of the books, articles, and studies mentioned in this bibliography are also mentioned in the text.

In compiling this bibliography, I have favored books devoted to dispassionate analysis of the strengths and weaknesses of American schools over books devoted to advocating a particular position. I have also included a great many books on the history of education. Most of the arguments about American education are quite old, and most of today's debaters have little understanding of how the structures of American education were created. The arguments of most debaters in education would be improved by a thorough study of the social history of American schools.

HISTORY

Raymond Callahan. *Education and the Cult of Efficiency.* Chicago: University of Chicago Press, 1962.

One of the classics of American educational history, Callahan's book analyzes how, between 1910 and 1920, prominent educators transformed schools from locally controlled institutions to massive centralized bureaucracies. It remains an unsurpassed account of the period.

Lawrence Cremin. *The Transformation of the School.* New York: Alfred A. Knopf, 1961.
Lawrence Cremin. *American Education: The Colonial Experience, 1607–1783.* New York: Harper & Row, 1970.
Lawrence Cremin. *American Education: The National Experience, 1783–1876.* New York: Harper & Row, 1980.
Lawrence Cremin. *American Education: The Metropolitan Experience, 1876–1980.* New York: Harper & Row, 1988.

American Education is the standard account of the history of American education; the second volume is the only book on the subject to win a Pulitzer. Toward the end of the series, Cremin devoted more space to ancillary subjects (the history of museums, publishing, the intellectual life) than to the schools. I suspect that this project began as a history of American education and ended as a history of American culture. Worth reading, but I wish it was less diffuse. *The Transformation of the School,* an early book that helped establish Cremin's reputation as a scholar, remains one of the best histories of the rise of progressive education.

Charles Glenn. *The Myth of the Common School.* Amherst: University of Massachusetts Press, 1987.
Charles Glenn. *Choice of Schools in Six Nations.* Washington, D.C.: U.S. Department of Education, 1990.

A long-time Massachusetts education bureaucrat who helped create Boston's school busing plan, Glenn made a successful mid-life career change to become an education historian at Boston University. *The Myth of the Common School* is the best source for information on how Horace Mann and his peers persuaded government officials and other concerned citizens in the United States, France, and elsewhere to make education a concern of the state. *Choice of Schools in Six Nations* provides short histories of school choice in France, Netherlands, Belgium, Britain, Canada, and Germany. A sequel describing the history of school choice in Eastern Europe is forthcoming.

Robert Hampel. *The Last Little Citadel.* Boston: Houghton Mifflin, 1986.

One of a series of books commissioned by the National Association of Secondary Schools and the National Association of Independent Schools in the mid-1980s (the other two being Theodore Sizer's *Horace's Compromise* and Arthur Powell, Eleanor Farrar, and David Cohen's *The Shopping Mall High School*). Hempel's book is a tightly written social history of American education since 1900. A valuable short book that conveys more information on this subject than much longer books by other authors. The citations are particularly valuable.

Lloyd Jorgenson. *The State and the Non-Public School, 1825–1925.* Lexington: University Press of Kentucky, 1987.

A thorough account of the attempts in the nineteenth and early twentieth century to suppress American private schools. A very vivid and lively history.

Diane Ravitch. *The Great School Wars.* New York: Basic Books, 1974.
Diane Ravitch. *The Troubled Crusade.* New York: Basic Books, 1983.

Now a Brookings Institution scholar, Ravitch's first career was as an education historian. *The Great School Wars* remains her best book, a superb account of the battles over

New York City schools over the past century. *The Troubled Crusade,* though described as a history of American education between 1945 and 1980, is actually a series of essays rather than a systematic history. Some of the essays, particularly those dealing with federal aid to education and with desegregation, are superb. A detailed history of American education since 1945 still needs to be written.

David Tyack. *The One Best System.* Cambridge, MA: Harvard University Press, 1974.
David Tyack and Elizabeth Hansot. *Managers of Virtue.* New York: Basic Books, 1982.
David Tyack. "The Perils of Pluralism." *American Historical Review,* October 1968.
David Tyack. "Pilgrim's Progress." *History of Education Quarterly,* Fall 1976.

The best American education historian. Tyack is particularly concerned with the changes in the first part of the twentieth century that transformed American education from a decentralized, locally controlled system into a rigid, centralized, hierarchical bureaucracy. *The One Best System* describes how the Progressives took over control of the schools and ensured that parents would have no say in how schools were run. *Managers of Virtue,* a sort of sequel, tells who the major Progressives were, how they networked, and how their ideas permanently transformed the schools. *The Perils of Pluralism* remains the most detailed account of the Supreme Court's *Pierce* decision that declared private schools constitutional. *Pilgrim's Progress* describes how the superintendent of schools changed between 1860 and 1960; it certainly could be expanded into a book that, if written, would be a useful addition to education history.

E. G. West. *Education and the Industrial Revolution.* New York: Barnes & Noble, 1975.

West, a noted Canadian economic historian, is best known as an expert on vouchers. But this book (his best) tells the story of how a small group of people in Britain successfully nationalized the schools in the nineteenth century. The British educational trends West chronicles parallel the American trends Charles Glenn describes in *The Myth of the Common School*.

SCHOOL ORGANIZATION AND STRUCTURE

Joseph Bast & Diane Bast, eds. *Rebuilding America's Schools.* Chicago: Heartland Institute, 1991.

Not actually a book, but a collection of eight reports in a loose-leaf binder on school choice. The best reports are Joseph Bast and Robert Wittmann's history of educational choice legislation and Wittmann's technical analysis of the differences between existing choice proposals. Bast and Wittmann also contribute a very useful bibliography.

Anthony S. Bryk, Valerie B. Lee, & Peter B. Holland. *Catholic Schools and the Common Good.* Cambridge, MA: Harvard University Press, 1993.

A book that complements and does not, for the most part, contradict the work of James Coleman and his associates, *Catholic Schools and the Common Good* is an excellent analysis of Catholic high schools. Part of the book is overly technical, as the authors manipulate data in ways most people will find confusing, but the first chapter on Catholic school history is excellent, and the authors' study of various Catholic schools also makes many sound points. The authors' conclusions, calling for government funding of Catholic schools but opposing school choice, are quite provocative.

John Chubb and Terry Moe. *Politics, Markets, and America's Schools.* Washington, D.C.: Brookings Institution, 1990.
John Chubb and Terry Moe. *A Lesson in School Reform from Great Britain.* Washington, D.C.: Brookings Institution, 1992.

Politics, Markets, and America's Schools is a severely flawed book. Many of the chapters are highly technical discussions of organizational theory that the average reader will find impenetrable. The authors' case for school choice, though celebrated, is much weaker and more dogmatic than might be expected. The book's great strength is that the authors, following in James Coleman's footsteps, gathered a great deal of data and conclusively proved that the school "reforms" of 1983 to 1985 did more harm than good. *Politics, Markets, and America's Schools* is far more important in its diagnosis of what is wrong with the schools than on how to improve them. *A Lesson in School Reform from Great Britain* is a short study (reprinted from the *London Sunday Times Magazine*) of British school reform that has interesting anecdotal information, but is not thorough or systematic.

James Coleman, Sally Kilgore, and Thomas Hoffer. *High School Achievement.* New York: Basic Books, 1982.
James Coleman and Thomas Hoffer. *Public and Private High Schools.* New York: Basic Books, 1987.

Much American educational research over the past quarter-century are footnotes to James Coleman's work. From the Coleman report of 1966, to his "white flight" research of the mid-1970s, to these two books, Coleman has been a pioneer in producing rigorous but controversial social science about education. Here Coleman and his collaborators explore the topic of why private high schools do a better job of educating students than their public counterparts. Difficult, but essential, reading.

John Coons and Stephen D. Sugarman. *Education by Choice.*
Berkeley, CA: University of California Press, 1978.

John Coons and Stephen D. Sugarman. *Scholarships for Children.* Berkeley, CA: Institute of Governmental Affairs,
University of California (Berkeley), 1992.

John Coons. "School Choice as Simple Justice." *First Things,*
April 1992.

> John Coons is a law professor at the University of
> California (Berkeley) who has campaigned in his home
> state and elsewhere for school choice as the most effective
> and democratic means of achieving desegregation and
> aiding the poor. *Education by Choice* remains the most
> extended philosophical treatment of how school choice
> would transform public education; its arguments and
> analyses have not been superseded by later discussions
> of the subject. "School Choice as Simple Justice" is a coda
> to *Education by Choice,* providing Coons's explanations as
> to how his views have changed over the years. *Scholarships for Children* is an analysis of the strengths and weaknesses of school choice proposals introduced between
> 1987 and 1992.

Nathan Glazer, ed. *The Public Interest on Education.* Cambridge,
MA: Abt Books, 1984.

> *The Public Interest* has been interested in education for
> over a quarter-century; many of the more important
> authors in the field, including Christopher Jencks, James
> Coleman, Thomas Sowell, and Charles Glenn, have published in the journal's pages. This book collects articles on
> a wide variety of topics, including Martin Eger on moral
> education, Sen. Daniel Patrick Moynihan on Supreme
> Court decisions affecting religious schools, and David K.
> Cohen and Eleanor Farrar on education vouchers. A *Public
> Interest* reader would be welcome.

Gerald Grant. *What We Learned at Hamilton High.* Cambridge, MA: Harvard University Press, 1988.

Grant tells the story of American education over the past quarter-century by describing how a typical urban high school changed over the past thirty years. Grant spent a year teaching in the school, collected anecdotal history about the school's past, and produced one of the most vivid books about high schools ever written. The first third is a history of "Hamilton High," and the remaining two-thirds are Grant's account of the organizational problems of high schools. Grant is a very compelling writer.

Paul T. Hill, Gail E. Foster and Tamar Gendler. *High Schools with Character.* Santa Monica, CA: RAND, 1990.

Paul T. Hill and Jacqueline Bonan. *Decentralization and Accountability in Public Education.* Santa Monica, CA : RAND, 1991.

RAND isn't usually thought of as an education think tank, but their papers on this subject have always been worth reading. *In High Schools with Character,* Paul Hill and colleagues look at the corporate culture of high schools to understand why they all too often lack meaning and purpose. *Decentralization and Accountability in Public Education* is the best critique of school-based management yet published.

Susan Moore Johnson. *Teachers Unions in Schools.* Philadelphia: Temple University Press, 1984.

Susan Moore Johnson. *Teachers at Work.* New York: Basic Books, 1990.

Johnson's area of expertise is the life of the teacher in the classroom, including the nonsense she has to deal with from her superiors and her students. *Teachers Unions in Schools* is the best source for learning how the unionization of schools in the 1960s and 1970s transformed them. *Teachers at Work* is a lengthy analysis of the frustrations teachers have to face and how these problems were created.

William K. Kilpatrick, *Why Johnny Can't Tell Right from Wrong.* New York: Simon & Schuster, 1992.

The problems of teaching morality in the school system are quite complex, and it is hard for a reader without a solid background in the history of educational psychology to understand why educators come up with the schemes that they have created. Kilpatrick, a professor of education at Boston University, has a solid understanding of psychologists and the psychological mindset, and conveys his knowledge in a sure and confident manner. Included in this book are discussions of the problems of sex education and drug education as well as an extensive annotated bibliography of good books that children should read. The best book on the problems of moral education in America yet written.

Edward Pauly. *The Classroom Crucible.* New York: Basic Books, 1991.

Pauly's thesis is a provocative one: None of the school reforms instituted over the past quarter-century have worked because teachers ignore commands imposed from above and teach any way they choose. His conclusions will certainly be debated, but one can hardly quibble with Pauly's analysis of why school reforms have failed. Pauly's discussion of how teachers establish control over their classrooms is also interesting.

Arthur Powell, Eleanor Farrar and David K. Cohen. *The Shopping Mall High School.* Boston: Houghton Mifflin, 1985.

One of a trio of studies commissioned by the National Association of Secondary School Principals and the National Association of Independent Schools in the mid-1980s, along with Robert Hampel's *The Last Little Citadel* and Theodore Sizer's *Horace's Compromise.* Powell's team visited a great many high schools and discovered that they were like shopping malls: Students were free to choose whatever they wanted, and no one was willing or able to tell them what was right or wrong. The authors are particularly good at finding telling anecdotes. Also included is David K. Cohen's thoughtful analysis of how curricula have been watered down over the past seventy-five years.

Gilbert Sewall. *Necessary Lessons.* New York: Free Press, 1983.

Now the director of the American Textbook Council, Sewall was formerly the education editor of *Newsweek* and one of the two directors of the Educational Excellence Network. *Necessary Lessons* is somewhat dated in its conclusions and in its reporting, but Sewall did a thorough job in finding and summarizing the most lasting educational research of the time. A valuable resource, and one of the models for this book.

Theodore R. Sizer. *Horace's School.* Boston: Houghton Mifflin, 1992.

I've excluded from this bibliography most of the books about schools (including *Horace's Compromise*, the predecessor to this volume) that are extended opinion pieces rather than dispassionate analysis, but the power of Sizer's writing cannot be ignored. Sizer is unusual in that he is both a traditionalist and a disciple of John Dewey, which makes him one of the few Americans who could be legitimately described as a progressive conservative (or a conservative progressive). His ideal high school would replace the existing curriculum with fewer, team-taught classes; instead of examinations, students would have to produce "exhibitions" demonstrating their intelligence and creativity. A quite provocative book; while his conclusions may not be persuasive, the questions Sizer asks about high schools are ones that most have ignored.

Thomas Toch. *In the Name of Excellence.* New York: Oxford University Press, 1991.

A book that attempts to summarize American education in the manner of Martin Mayer's *The Schools* or Charles Silberman's *Crisis in the Classroom.* Much of the book does not succeed because Toch spends too much time describing inside-the-Beltway education mandarins whose policies ultimately had little influence. But two chapters are worth reading: Toch's analysis of the problems of testing and his reporting on the lobbying of teachers' unions, a surprisingly hard-hitting section. The remaining portions of *In the Name of Excellence* plow familiar fields.

Perry A. Zirkel and Sharon Nalbone Richardson. *A Digest of Supreme Court Decisions Affecting Education.* 2nd edition. Bloomington, IN: Phi Delta Kappa Educational Foundation, 1988.

One of the books about education that needs to be written is a history of the courts and the schools, showing how Supreme Court decisions have affected conduct, culture, and performance. Until a comprehensive book is written, Zirkel and Richardson's treatise is the best book on the subject. It is a summary of all major Supreme Court decisions affecting the schools; each decision includes the vote, the case history, and the Court's findings. While a very dry book, the *Digest* is nonetheless a handy guide to sorting out the Supreme Court's arcane rulings on the schools.

INDEX

tion Association (NEA);
United Federation of
Teachers
Thatcher, Margaret, 127, 165
Thernstrom, Abagail, 158
Thomas Jefferson Research
Center, 37
Thompson, William Hale (Big
Bill), 98
Timar, Thomas, 108
Tinker v. Des Moines, xii, 51–52
Toch, Thomas, 80
trade schools, ix–x, 7–8
Troen, Selwyn K., 91
Truman administration, x, 17
tuition tax credit concept, 149,
153–154
Turner, W. W., 2
Tyack, David, 52, 89, 92, 95, 97

United Federation of Teachers,
19–20, 50, 102–103
U. S. Department of Education: creation of, x, 21–22;
proposals to limit, 136

values: decline in high-school
student, 38; movement to
clarify, xi, 31–32; teaching of, 34–36, 40–41
Values Education Commis-
sion, Maryland, 35–36
Van Wyck, Sylvanus, 90
violence, school, 73–74
vocational schools. *See* education spending, federal;
trade schools

voucher system: external
voucher plan, 155–156;
Great Britain, xvii, 165;
Milwaukee, xvi, 141–142,
145, 160–163; origins of
and response to, 147–149;
school choice test pro-
gram, 18–19

ward boards, xiv, 88-91. *See
also* boards of education,
local
Welsh, Patrick, 76–77, 113
Whitney, Frank P., 49
Whitten, Jamie, 146
Whitty, Geoff, 166
Wildavsky, Ben, 161
Williams, Polly, 161
Wilson, Henry, 6
Wilson, Steven F., 125, 158
Wirt, Frederick, 49
Wirth, Arthur G., 9–10
Witte, John F., 162
*Witters v. Washington Depart-
ment of Services for the
Blind,* 154
Wittman, Robert, 145, 169–170
Wood v. Strickland, 53
Wynne, Edward, 35, 36

Young, Ella Flagg, xv, 119–120
Yulish, Stephen, 28

*Zobrest v. Catalina Foothills
School District,* 154
Zorach v. Clawson, 151